Martin Luther King's
Beloved Community
**begins with words
and
culminates in action**

I was recently reminded of the Rev. Dr.'s ability to write and speak words that held a mirror up to power while telling immutable truths. He did not do this alone, but while standing at the center of a strong community — one cultivated over many years before his most iconic speeches and civil rights actions.

How can we cultivate our own community, one in which we feel connected, supported, and strong? Are there concrete steps forward? How do we even get started?

The book in your hands is not as much about how to improve your writing, as about how writing can improve your connections.

Heartspoken:
**How to Write Notes
that Connect, Comfort,
Encourage, and Inspire**

In it, the handwritten note emerges from old-fashioned irrelevance to become a powerful tool. *Heartspoken* will help you uncover your own unique writing voice... *and* give you the confidence to use it.

Consider a light switch. When it's flipped one can't see the electricity and may not even understand how it works — but the flowing power is nothing short of a miracle.

Elizabeth's "NOTES" formula shows how to find and flip that switch in your own writing — opening the door to belonging, gratitude, and impact.

In 2024 and beyond, may this book make your writing more alive and meaningful — both to you and for others!

www.newground.net

Celebrating 30 Years of Connecting Money with What Matters ℠

"Elizabeth Cottrell is renowned for her letter writing. I have been the recipient of many of her heartwarming notes over the years. She has taken this expertise and put it into a practical guide for writing notes that touch the heart. If you want to write letters that people hang on to and cherish, this is the book for you."

—**Marnie Pehrson Kuhns,** Best-Selling Author and Blogger at CreationGirl.com and MarnieKuhns.com

"Elizabeth H. Cottrell's heart for encouragement takes the shape of words penned in notes and cards and letters—sometimes considered an old-fashioned way to communicate in our fast-paced world of email and texts. I'm so grateful she's inspired me to slow down and reconnect with family and friends through the more personal expression of handwritten notes."

—**Beth K. Vogt,** Award-Winning Author at bethvogt.com

"I have known Elizabeth for over a decade, and her message has never wavered—she lives on connections with her faith, with others, with herself, and with nature. Elizabeth has produced the definitive note-writing resource. If you want to write more handwritten notes—and do it well—invest in this book."

—**Karen R. Sanderson,** Author of *No Boundaries*

"*Heartspoken* is the answer to my note-writing struggle. From the first time we met ten years ago, her message has been about writing notes from the heart. Being privy to the evolution of this book, I know her inspirational words and pragmatic advice will help struggling note writers like me find the right words to connect more deeply with those we care about. This book will be sitting on my desk when I need help crafting my next heartspoken note."

—**Denise Wakeman,** Founder, Marketing Trailblazers Community

Praise for
Heartspoken:
How to Write Notes That Connect,
Comfort, Encourage, and Inspire

Many of the following are excerpted from longer testimonials that can be found at the bottom of the author's book page on her website: https://heartspoken.com/heartspoken-book.

"What you have in your hand is far more than another book on the proper way to write a note or letter. It offers you the inspiration and encouragement to know—deep in your soul—exactly the right thing to say at the right time."

—**Jason F. Wright,** *New York Times* Best-Selling Author of
Christmas Jars, The Wednesday Letters, and *Even the Dog Knows*
jasonfwright.com

"This book is a gift. . . . As a business etiquette expert, I have been teaching people the value of writing notes as a tool for growing their business and building relationships. Elizabeth has gone farther, deeper, and wider. Elizabeth has created one of the most valuable books you'll ever own and will refer to over and over for years to come."

—**Lydia Ramsey,** Business Etiquette and
Modern Manners Expert
LydiaRamsey.com

"In a contemporary culture where civility among humans sometimes lapses, *Heartspoken* is a timely reminder of its benefits. Ms. Cottrell polishes the old tool of note writing to suggest how easily we can positively affect the lives of others. The emotional return possible from the few moments invested in a well-timed note is compelling. The author's primer . . . is a relevant document for compassionate people of all ages."

—**E. A. Coe,** Author of Four Books, Including
The Other Side of Good
www.eacoe.online

"Over the years, Elizabeth has blessed me with her handwritten notes, both in times of sorrow and in times of joy. . . . If anyone can bring back the lost art of the letter, it's Elizabeth Cottrell. Her book is your instruction manual in making our world a kinder, more compassionate, and thoughtful place. God knows, we need this in our lives now more than ever!"

—**Ellen Britt,** PA, EdD

"In this book, Elizabeth Cottrell shows how to develop your superpower of writing heart-to-heart notes. Her NOTES formula is a great way to get started, and you'll find plenty of situation-specific tips within these pages as well. With this book by your side, you can become a world-class note writer, engendering good feelings in others' lives as well as your own!"

—**Lynette M. Smith,** Author of *How to Write Heartfelt Letters to Treasure: For Special Occasions and Occasions Made Special*

"In a world where connectedness is defined by social media likes and instant messages, Elizabeth Cottrell reminds us of the benefits of pausing to pen a heartspoken personal note, both for the writer and the recipient. With her easy-to-remember and employ NOTES formula, Cottrell inspires amateurs and experienced letter writers alike to express compassion and caring with thoughtful words. A lovely gift for a teen, young professional, aspiring leader, and even the veteran snail mail aficionado."

—**Ann Davison,** Executive Coach and Strategic
Communications Advisor

"*Heartspoken* is not just an inspiring how-to book that will enable you to write meaningful notes that other people will cherish; it is heartspoken itself. Cottrell writes from an open and authentic soul, empowering you to speak your own heart."

—**Cara Achterberg,** Author of Seven Books, Including
National Best-Seller *Girls' Weekend* and
Memoir *Another Good Dog*
www.carawrites.com

"'Delightful' is the word that comes to mind when reading Elizabeth H. Cottrell's *Heartspoken*. It is a combination of etiquette, common sense, and exquisite advice on how to write the perfect note or letter. . . . It is full of examples, and replete with quotes from history's greatest letter writers. Most of all, it is a spiritual guide for communing with others on a heartfelt, heartspoken level."

—**Dana Hayward,** Author of *Entropy*

"An artist creates a painting with canvas, color, and brushes. The finished canvas evokes feelings which are revisited with each viewing. Elizabeth is an artist with words that evoke a feeling in the heart. This book she has written gives us the tools to create personal notes that also become works of art that we can be sure will be treasured."

—**Pamela McRae-Dux,** Author and Publisher, Simple Books

"Oh, how we need this book by Elizabeth Cottrell. Cottrell does an amazing job detailing those ways in which we can share heart and soul in our handwritten notes. Cottrell's book is a great gift to yourself and to others who appreciate the power of heartspoken mail."

—**Pamela S Wight,** Author of Romantic Suspense (*The Right Wrong Man, Twin Desires*), Children's Books (*Birds of Paradise, Molly Finds Her Purr*), and a Flash Memoir (*Flashes of Life*)

"Elizabeth Cottrell and I share a belief in the power of a piece of mail to connect, comfort, encourage, and inspire—to create and strengthen that which is most important: human relationships. I recommend reading her book on how, when, and why to send a personal note, to help you harness this power. Most importantly, I encourage you to send a heartspoken card or note to a loved one; the impact of that effort is likely greater than anything else you will do today!"

—**George White,** President of Up With Paper and Past President, Greeting Card Association

"This book is a delightful outpouring of Elizabeth's passion to share the power of handwritten correspondence to enhance lives of senders and recipients. It's a passion that we share in her Facebook group: The Art of the Heartspoken Note. For graduating students and new professionals, *Heartspoken* makes a great gift to learn how to make an impression and cultivate the ability to build relationships. This book will help you write any note so you are sure to convey your sincere appreciation to your loved ones, colleagues, friends, and even strangers as a lifelong practice full of rich rewards."

—**Jan Carroza,** Center for Direct Marketing: dmcenter. com, Author of *Rockin' ROI: How to Bootstrap Ecommerce with Performance-Based Marketing*

"This comprehensive guide shows when, how, and why to put hand to paper. Eight chapters cover every aspect of personal and professional letter writing with lots of valuable examples. With her compassionate guidance, you'll feel like there is suddenly a quill in your hand, capable of writing with old-fashioned, graceful sensibilities."

—**Annette Petrick,** Writer and Radio Personality,
Author of *Christmas Joy, Love & Wonder*
ConsiderThisRadioshow.com

"Elizabeth Cottrell is the perfect person to have written this book. It was over a decade ago when I first met her in person. I was a new speaker at an event in Atlanta, and she and I ended up sitting at the same table for lunch. During this brief encounter, Elizabeth put me at ease, and my nervousness and fear dissipated. Thank you, Elizabeth, and I am forever grateful to be connected with you."

—**Connie Ragen Green,** Author and Marketing Strategist
ConnieRagenGreen.com

"As an enthusiastic supporter of handwritten notes, I welcome the publication of Elizabeth H. Cottrell's *Heartspoken: How to Write Notes that Connect, Comfort, Encourage, and Inspire.* Not only does she state a clear case for the charms and benefits of the handwritten note, she provides tools to address any fears related to the writing of them. Handwritten notes provide a window to the soul that email and emojis cannot open. In a complicated and challenging world, they bring affirmation that someone cared enough to write and took the time to do so. They are a gift of immeasurable worth."

—**Jill P. Strachan,** Author of *Waterfalls, the Moon, and Sensible Shoes: One Lesbian Life*

"I love Elizabeth Cottrell's book and her commonsense, heartfelt advice about sending notes and letters in the mail. She is absolutely spot on in her message. Receiving a heartspoken note or letter in the mail can make a huge impact in someone's life. It's on my gift-giving list this year!"

—**Lois Carter Crawford,** Author of *It Ain't Just the Diet COOKBOOK: How I Beat Food Allergies One Bite At a Time*; *It Ain't Just the Diet FOOD JOURNAL: A Daily Guide to Finding & Managing Your Food Allergies*; and *Secrets of the Softer Side of Selling*

"Congratulations on the book, Elizabeth. In this crazy world, every little thing that connects us in a real way, that nurtures our humanity, is such a gift. Letters from the heart are just that."

—**Shawn MacKENZIE,** Author of *Tarot of Dragons* and *Llewellyn's Little Book of Dragons*

Heartspoken: How to Write Notes that Connect,
Comfort, Encourage, and Inspire

by Elizabeth H. Cottrell

ISBN 978-1-64663-724-9

Published by

köehlerbooks™

3705 Shore Drive
Virginia Beach, VA 23455
800-435-4811
www.koehlerbooks.com

HEART
SPOKEN

How to Write Notes that
Connect, Comfort, Encourage, and Inspire

ELIZABETH H.
COTTRELL

Foreword by Jason F. Wright
New York Times Bestselling Author of *Christmas Jars* and *The Wednesday Letters*

VIRGINIA BEACH
CAPE CHARLES

To my mother, Elizabeth Thomson Herbert,
who taught me the importance of writing notes and always made me
feel I could do anything . . . even write a book.

To my daughter, Sarah Cottrell Propst,
who believed in me, encouraged me, and challenged me to write this
book. You are a gift to me in so many ways.

To my husband, John Austin Cottrell, Jr.,
whose love for me and support for this project have been unflagging.

TABLE OF CONTENTS

FOREWORD

T hreaded throughout my work over many years has been my love for the long-lost art of the handwritten note or letter— those personal notes we used to write, address, stuff, seal, stamp, and send.

Many of our children have no idea how exciting it can be to receive a real letter in the mail. They haven't experienced the power of opening the mailbox with its distinctive squeak, peeking inside, pulling out the stacks of bills and catalogs, and finding a gem.

Remember discovering an envelope with your name on it? Written by hand? Maybe it was from your grandmother, a sibling in the military, an old teacher, that friend you met at summer camp.

I wrote and received lots of letters like that as a kid. I recall riding the bus home from school, sitting on those green seats, sticky duct tape hiding the holes, staring out the window and praying I'd have a letter in the black metal mailbox at the bottom of our long, winding, gravel driveway.

And when I did? I sat on a stump in the woods near the house or next to our small creek and tore open the envelope. The smile lasted until bedtime.

No doubt some of you can relate.

There's simply something special about these personal gifts of words on paper. The writer isn't just sending you bits of news, encouragement, or love; they're giving you time and a piece of themselves.

The beauty is found in much more than the words. It's in the process. The hand sweeping across the page. The pause to reflect, to reread, to fix a misshapen *l, m, n,* or *p.*

A letter is more than ink and paper. It's heart and soul.

Emails? Texts? Facebook messages? They can be beautiful blessings. But tech can't replace the purity of a piece of paper, a pen, a few minutes, and a little love.

What you have in your hand is far more than another book on the proper way to write a note or letter. It is written with care and commitment to build your confidence and teach you to find your own "voice." It offers you the inspiration and encouragement to know—deep in your soul—exactly the right thing to say at the right time.

For Elizabeth Cottrell, writing notes is a true ministry, and she practices what she teaches. I know that's true, because my family and I—and no doubt hundreds of others—have been fortunate recipients of her notes of encouragement and comfort over the years.

The forced isolation of the COVID-19 pandemic has shown us our desperate need for genuine connection. Notes and letters written from the heart are surely among the most powerful—and affordable—connection tools we have.

Read *HEARTSPOKEN: How to Write Notes that Connect, Comfort, Encourage, and Inspire* and let's keep this movement going!

I'll be waiting at the mailbox.

Jason Wright

PO Box 669

Woodstock, Virginia 22664

Jason F. Wright is a New York Times *bestselling author of* Christmas Jars, The Wednesday Letters, *and his just-released* Even the Dog Knows. *Jason is also a columnist and speaker. Learn more at jasonfwright.com.*

PREFACE
The Heartspoken Promise

The heart can speak when oft the tongue is mute.
Our sighs and longings wait to be expressed . . .
So trust your still small voice to speak them true,
And know heartspoken words are ever blessed.

~ Elizabeth H. Cottrell

A letter from a stranger was the lightning bolt that changed my appreciation for the potential of personal notes forever; from that day on, I saw them as a force for good in the world.

I've always written notes, because that's what we were taught to do when I was growing up in the 1950s. I learned the skill from my mother and both my grandmothers. They all wrote beautiful notes. It was expected. It was good manners.

But the day I received that letter, I suddenly realized it was so much more.

The letter was from a woman devastated by the loss of her son:

"I truly appreciated the encouraging letter you sent my son's fiancée after my son took his own life. She shared it with me, and it came during one of the most difficult and testing times of my life. I know

I have read your note over 25 times; it was a lifeline which kept my spirits up."

What on earth had I written that could have meant so much to this woman? Her son's fiancé was a neighbor of mine and only a casual acquaintance. I only remember, upon hearing the news of this man's tragic death, that I wanted desperately to reach out to her and let her know she was not alone. To this day, I have no idea what I wrote, but I know it came from my heart and carried a genuine desire to comfort her.

On reading the mother's anguished missive, I remember experiencing a moment of instant clarity: a note crafted with thoughtfulness and compassion can have impact and create a ripple effect. I've been a believer in the power of note writing ever since.

I do not use the word "power" lightly.

As I began sharing my enthusiasm for note writing and encouraging others to help me revive the lost art, I heard more and more stories of notes and letters (notes just being shorter in length than letters) that made a difference by connecting, comforting, encouraging, or inspiring. I was surprised to learn how many of my friends lacked the confidence that would enable them to be regular note writers.

"I wish I could write notes more easily."

"I never know what to say."

"I'm afraid I'll say the wrong thing."

This book is for all those friends. And this book is for you if you

- would like note writing to be easier, quicker, and more fun

- want to write more personal notes but can't seem to find your own voice to do it

- want confidence and ideas about what to say in a note, especially when the situation is awkward or laden with deep emotion

- want to learn how note writing can become a powerful communication tool in your professional life

- want to learn about notes that have impacted lives

- need the perfect gift for anyone who is a natural connector or dedicated note writer

I will show you how to reframe the writing of notes, slip into an artistic, creative flow, and pull inspiration and energy from beyond yourself.

Consider the flipping of a light switch. You can't see the electricity. You may not even understand how it works. But when power starts flowing through the open wire, it is nothing short of miraculous. I want to show you how to find and flip that switch in your own note writing.

Grasp this beautiful process, and your writing will become alive, meaningful, and impactful in ways you could never have thought possible. You'll become part of a long and illustrious epistolic heritage.

Some say the handwritten note is a dying art; yet in both professional and personal life, it is still one of the most powerful tools we have for connecting meaningfully with others. A well-written note can give voice to the stirrings of your most heartfelt sentiments and can be read, saved, and treasured forever. While I am passionate about the special gift of a handwritten note sent by mail, this book will help you write any kind of note—personal or professional, handwritten or typed—with more energy and impact. With more heart.

Whether you are comforting a friend who has lost a loved one, congratulating a coworker on a job promotion, or thanking a potential boss for an interview, this power comes through your heart and out through your pen onto paper. Your note's reader feels this same energy at the other end. Sometimes it's just a small warmth . . . sometimes a glow . . . sometimes a blazing flame. But when you make your words *heartspoken*, you change a simple piece of paper to an affirmation, a hug, a pat on the back, a comforting touch, an encouraging pep talk, or an expression of sympathy, love, or gratitude.

Stop wondering *how* to do it, for I believe you will quickly master writing short, simple notes that connect, comfort, encourage, and inspire.

Once you learn how to make your notes heartspoken, they are no longer an obligation—they're a privilege and a joy.

Elizabeth H. Cottrell

CHAPTER I
Before You Begin

"Words can travel thousands of miles.
May my words create mutual understanding and love.
May they be as beautiful as gems,
As lovely as flowers."

~ Thich Nhat Hanh

This Book's Birthing:
From My Heart to
Your Hands

Ideas, like seeds, can sometimes take a long time to reach fruition. Over ten years ago, I created the *Heartspoken* blog to encourage readers and share my belief in strengthening what I consider the four essential connections of a heartspoken life: with God (faith), with others (connection), with self (self-knowledge), and with nature. The research I did to nourish these essential connections in my own life led me to information and wisdom, not the least of which were findings by neuroscientists that we humans are *hardwired* for connection.

Handwritten notes have been effective, meaningful tools for connection throughout my life. Writing expressions of support, encouragement, love, and gratitude came naturally to me, and I have been so touched, even surprised, by the responses of those who received my missives. Soon after her father died, my friend Shelia rushed up to me after church. *"Daddy had a whole basket of cards and notes he kept to reread,"* she said with tears in her eyes. *"Several of them were from you, and I want you to know how much they meant to him and to our whole family!"*

Other stories are potent reminders of the difference a single note or letter can mean in someone's life. Author Jason Wright lives down the road from me and has featured letters in many of his popular books. His appreciation for a well-crafted letter is genuine and came from an excruciatingly painful time in his own life when, as a teenager, he lost his father. One of his teachers wrote him an encouraging letter that touched him so deeply that he has carried it with him ever since, pulling it out to read when he needs encouragement.

This book's title, *Heartspoken,* came to me years before I ever wrote a word. I knew I could write notes that seemed to touch those to whom I was writing, and I was hearing from others who wanted to know my secret. But a negative gremlin kept popping up, trying to convince me the world didn't need another book on how to write notes. It's a lost art anyway, right?

But COVID-19 changed everything.

As I write this, we are still in the grip of this global pandemic, a crisis forcing every one of us to redefine what connection looks like in our lives when we can't be together safely in the same room. Suddenly, across the country, there is a resurgent interest in note and letter writing.

We're writing to family and friends.

We're writing to those who are sick.

We're writing to children and grandchildren whose lives have been turned upside down by school closures.

We're writing to fellow church members since we can't gather in our churches.

We're writing to residents of nursing homes who aren't allowed to leave or have visitors.

We're writing to healthcare heroes who are risking their own lives for their patients.

We're writing to law enforcement officers and firefighters who risk their lives to keep us safe.

We're writing to loved ones because we're suddenly aware we might die sooner than we thought.

We're writing because amid these surreal circumstances, personal notes seem more real and more important than they ever have before. And as my friend Heather shared with me, "There are times—especially when we are reaching out to someone who has had a devastating loss— when email does not suffice, texting does not suffice, e-cards do not suffice . . . even store-bought cards do not suffice."

Only a personal, heartspoken letter will do.

As I was dealing with the angst of having a milestone birthday in the middle of COVID-19's "Great Pause," my daughter Sarah urged me—challenged me, actually—to write this book, a book she's heard me talk about for years. The timing was right; the silver lining of this pandemic was not only the cancellation of many other commitments but also the renewed appreciation for the important relationships in our lives—the ones we need to cultivate and cherish.

And as I faced my own mortality, I suddenly realized if I'm not going to write this book now, then when? The world may have other books on note writing, but it doesn't have *my* book on note writing. It doesn't have a book with my own secret formula for writing heartspoken notes.

In writing this book, I want to share my conviction that notes— especially handwritten notes—are a beautiful and overlooked connection tool, often the best choice when we want our connection to be especially rich, intimate, and meaningful. I want to give you the confidence to reach down deep into your heart to write your own words that connect, comfort, encourage, and inspire.

A Brief History of Note Writing

I n ancient times, we humans left our words and symbols on cave walls and tablets of stone and copper, but it wasn't until the advent of paper—especially papyrus paper—that we had the means to share our words more easily and broadly. Papyrus paper became the most popular conveyance of information in the world for more than 4,000 years, and much of it was surprisingly durable. Fragments of papyrus from around 3,000 BC have been found in Egypt's Pharaonic tombs, though these earliest writings were more often lists or inventories or funerary scrolls than personal missives. Personal correspondence came much later, as documented in remnants of notes written by Persian Queen Atossa in about 500 BC.

The Greeks began to use parchment (processed animal skin) around the second century BC, but it seems to have been used more for manuscripts than for any kind of personal correspondence. The origins of paper as we know it today began in first-century China, where it was made from macerated vegetables and other kinds of fiber. Chinese rice paper, made from strips cut from the pith of the rice paper tree, was popular in the sixth and seventh centuries.

In the late eighteenth and early nineteenth centuries, more modern paper made from wood pulp gained traction as automatic paper machines made paper more accessible and affordable. This meant letter writing was no longer limited to royalty and clergy.

History is full of great letter writers. In their correspondence, Pliny the Elder and Pliny the Younger recorded some of the gruesome details of the 79 AD eruption of Mt. Vesuvius. The venerable Bede, writing in the seventh century, was a prolific scribbler from the Dark Ages, and Queen Victoria embraced the art form and left us with many musings on life and politics in nineteenth-century England. John and Abigail Adams's lively correspondence gave us a glimpse into their world in the early years of the United States of America. In the twentieth century, Eleanor Roosevelt wrote thousands of intimate notes and letters, and George Bush is said to have written notes every day signed, *"All the best."*

According to the United States Postal Service, personal letters to the average home dropped from once every two weeks in 1987 to once every seven weeks in only twenty-three years. The downward trend in household first-class mail has continued year after year. No wonder those personal notes and letters are so special . . . they're so rare!

For centuries, historians have mined personal correspondence, looking for details of life, love, politics, and world events—sources of information to corroborate what they've learned elsewhere. What will future historians have to go on if we stop writing notes and letters?

How To Use This Book

Think of this book as more than a primer on how to write notes with impact. You can find any number of etiquette authorities who will tell you when it's appropriate to write certain notes and exactly what they think you should (and shouldn't) say. I've consulted many of these experts while researching material for this book, and I've included the basics of what you need to know to be a proficient note writer. For convenience and inspiration—to prime the pump of your note writing, if you will—I've also included ideas, examples, and suggestions for those especially challenging or unusual circumstances. I invite you to snag some of your favorites and claim them as your own.

But what I especially want to do here is teach you how to pause, breathe deeply, set your intention, and listen to your own inner voice to find words and emotions you know are uniquely yours. Once you've grasped that simple process, you'll never have to worry again about what to say or how to say it. You'll simply be opening the tap and letting your heart send its message. Whether you get a reply to your note or not, you can trust it will be just what is needed.

To help you navigate through this book as smoothly as possible, I have organized it into six main sections:

- Chapter I sets the stage with why I wrote the book, offering a bit of historical perspective and guidelines for using the book for maximum benefit.

- Chapter II helps you understand why connection matters and why cultivating the art of writing a heartspoken note is worth your time.

- Chapter III unveils the secret NOTES formula for any note and helps you tap into inspiration and energy to write those heartspoken words. This formula is the foundation of everything else in the book.

- Chapter IV explores how to apply the secret NOTES formula to your most common note-writing moments. Here you'll find sample sentences to use until you find your own voice.

- Chapter V offers examples of notes for less common situations, including some of the most oddball, awkward, or difficult ones I've ever had to write.

- Chapter VI shows you how to apply the principles in this book to business and professional correspondence.

- Chapter VII includes tools and tips for making your note writing easier and more fun.

By the final send-off in chapter VIII, you'll be ready to create your own note-writing legacy. With the resources and checklists in the appendices, you can't go wrong.

I've sprinkled in stories about the power of writing notes and letters throughout the book, but I've shared even more on this book's resource page: https://heartspoken.com/heartspoken-book-resources.

Learning any new skill is a process, not achieved instantaneously, but I think you'll find the pace easy and intuitive. I suggest you proceed cover to cover, front to back, so you can learn the secret NOTES formula for writing heartspoken notes and get familiar with the specific subtleties of different kinds of notes. Then the book can become a reference to be dipped into whenever you need specific help or inspiration—or be handed to a friend in need.

Please don't let yourself get overwhelmed! Wherever you are in your note-writing practice, commit to micro-steps toward the goal of becoming a more active note writer.

CHAPTER II
Start with WHY

"Great leaders are those who trust their gut. They are those who understand the art before the science. They win hearts before minds. They are the ones who start with WHY."

~ Simon Sinek

Words Touch Hearts and Lives

Commitment and intention are important ingredients for the attainment of any worthwhile accomplishment, but perhaps it's even more important to identify your WHY:

- Why do I want to write better notes?
- Why is it worth the effort?
- Why does it make a difference?

The answer to these questions will be unique to each of us, but for me, the answer is because I believe words—whether written by hand or typed on a keyboard—have the power to touch hearts and lives. The ability to write words that connect, comfort, encourage, and inspire is the closest we're likely to come in this lifetime to having a superpower. And as every superhero knows, their powers must be claimed, appreciated, and used.

My paternal grandfather, Robert Beverley Herbert, was seventy-one years old when I was born in 1950. Tucked inside the desk I've had since childhood, there is a well-worn and treasured bundle of letters he mailed me. The earliest was written when I was about seven years old, and they continued until I was twenty-two and he was ninety-three. These were the first meaningful letters I ever received, and they contained news, advice, and wisdom from a man who was born only fourteen years after Lee surrendered to Grant at Appomattox. Such is the connection power of words that they can cross centuries, miles, and even lifetimes.

Since those first treasured letters, I've received hundreds of beautiful messages in the form of handwritten notes and letters from friends, loved ones, and even strangers: congratulations when I reached milestones in my life; appreciation for things I've done or given; sympathy when I've experienced a loss; encouragement in the midst of a challenge; offers to help when I was heavily burdened; and "thinking of you" notes for no particular reason.

I've saved the most special of these notes and reread them often. Of course, any note from my husband and my children and their spouses is treasured correspondence. I consider each a precious gift with value far beyond the cost of the paper and postage.

My own WHY is because I want to make others feel as loved as I felt when I received one of these notes in the mail. This has moved me to do everything I can to revive the art of personal note and letter writing and encourage others to see what a powerful connection tool it is.

Not just because it's a nice thing to do (*but it is*).

Not just because it's often proper etiquette (*although it is*).

Absolutely not because I want to send anyone on a guilt trip (*but if you feel guilty because you think you should be writing more notes, stop right now. It won't help. Go get your pen and paper and start writing!*).

No, the reason I'm committed to shining a spotlight on the personal, handwritten note is because I believe notes containing words from your heart—*heartspoken*, written by hand, stamped, and mailed—are so much more meaningful than most emails or social media posts. We mustn't ignore such a simple and beautiful way to connect.

Writing a heartspoken note is not hard. You, too, can claim this superpower for yourself.

Begin with the Feeling

Take a few moments to reflect on notes and letters you've received over your lifetime. Perhaps you're remembering a love note, a sympathy note, or a "You've got this and I believe in you" note. Even if an epic story doesn't come to mind, I'll bet there was a memory or two you thought of when I mentioned it. Maybe you've got a frayed, folded note in your wallet, or maybe it's tucked away in your desk drawer or in a box with your most treasured possessions.

Or maybe you're not one to keep such things, but you have heart-memories of them.

Whether you still have a physical piece of paper or not, it's the *feeling* you most likely recall, not the exact words. And that feeling represents the love, care, kindness, and thoughtfulness conveyed by the sender.

So, if you want to learn how to write a note with impact, start by connecting with your own feelings for the person or the situation you're addressing. This connection will open the flow that conveys those feelings when your note is read.

And the recipient will know—even before they read the first word—you cared enough to take the time to gather your thoughts and send them in written form.

Connection Matters

D r. Brené Brown said it perfectly: *"Connection is why we're here. It's what gives purpose and meaning to our lives."* I believe our connection with others is a conduit for God's love, and scripture from various faith traditions would echo this conviction. I truly believe love is what life is all about, so you can understand why I get so excited about a simple, affordable tool that uses words written on paper to connect and share love with others quickly and easily.

Across cultural and socioeconomic lines, research from sociologists, psychologists, and mental health professionals confirms that connection is part of our "hardwiring" and matters greatly to our sense of well-being. A person who cultivates meaningful and healthy connections with others is likely to be happier, healthier, and more resilient in the face of adversity than someone who doesn't. Since sharing a piece of yourself through a note—handwritten or otherwise—is a highly effective connection tool, you are nourishing not only your own well-being but also your note recipient's.

In an article on her website, Rozanne Lopez echoes my sentiments about letters and notes: *"There is an excitement in receiving a letter in the mail, especially one without a specific reason attached to it. It is merely a good thought materialized and delivered physically into your hands. There is almost an alive and deeply intentional quality to a handwritten letter that is not existent in an email or a text."*

To get beyond basic letter-writing etiquette, I'm calling on you to reframe your perception of note writing. Think of it not as an obligation but as an opportunity and an investment in your relationships. Think of it as good karma! There is a spiritual element to a personal note that goes far beyond simple words on paper. Your heartspoken notes are divine threads of connection.

Sending an email or making a phone call is often quicker and easier than writing a note, and technology has swept us into an age where "snail mail" may seem antiquated or irrelevant. Every day, I use technology, send emails, and make phone calls, but when I write a note or letter and send it by mail, it tells someone I cared enough to spend one of the only nonrenewable resources I have—my time. Writer Philip Hensher expressed this so well: *"[Handwriting] involves us in a relationship with the written word which is sensuous, immediate, and individual."*

Your note to someone will stand out because everything else in their mailbox is likely to be marketing mail. If you can summon words from your heart that go beyond the expected, the generic, and the trite, then you will not just send a message, you will create a sacred experience.

Prolonged Impact

A s I've spoken to hundreds of friends and acquaintances about their thoughts on note writing, I've been surprised and moved by how often notes and letters are kept, preserved, and cherished.

"I've got a stash of handwritten letters and notes I've received. I love to pull them out and reread them."

"Every note I received after Joe died was like getting a hug. I've kept them to remind me how much he is still alive in the hearts and minds of so many."

"Seeing my father's handwriting on his letters makes me feel closer to him now that he's gone."

"When I open my mother's letters, there's a lingering scent of her perfume that takes me right back to my childhood and makes me feel her presence."

My good friend Esther is a particularly ardent believer in the power of handwritten notes, as you can read in her lovely comments:

"Elizabeth, I've been going through stacks of old cards and letters lately. Oh my . . . the things I'd forgotten! The gratitude people showed me that meant little at the time! The concern that friends had when I needed them most. All of it there in their handwriting. There are many friends' letters that I don't even have to look for signatures because I recognize their handwriting immediately. That handwriting itself is like seeing an old friend, and it is as individual as a person's voice. When I read my college friend's agony over a long-ago issue and read her responses to me, I hear them in her voice. When I read my college roommate's letters, in very different handwriting, I hear her calming, measured tones. My mother's beautiful handwriting brings back the warmth of her love and her pride in me. And so on . . . several notes from a man old enough to be my grandfather when he was my patient on a mental health ward, and I was still a student therapist. I didn't even remember that he had written to me. I've always been a believer in handwritten letters but had forgotten just how meaningful they can be."

Rabbi and author Elana Zaiman speaks of the letters she has received and saved throughout her life:

"On days when I feel out of sorts, I return to these letters. They strengthen me when I don't believe in myself, remind me who I am when I question my purpose or my values, and enable me to better reflect on my relationships and on my life . . . I experience a sense of gratitude for the love, concern, appreciation, compassion, kindness, wisdom, guidance, and honesty that many of these letters impart . . . and toward the people who took the time to write them."

Whether a note is handwritten or typed, when it is written, tucked into an envelope, addressed, stamped, and mailed, the physical component significantly adds to its impact on both the sender and the receiver.

For the beneficiary of our mailed correspondence, a note or letter becomes a gift to be enjoyed, saved, and treasured. Neither an email nor even a phone call will accomplish this. They can't compete at all.

It's Good for You

A colleague who counsels clients about their relationships helped me understand yet another benefit of handwritten notes and letters:

"From the writer's perspective, handwriting connects the emotional center of the brain with the logical parts of the brain, completing communication. Texting and emailing only engage the logic and reasoning area of the front brain, thus creating a bullet-point type of communication, removing connection, and disengaging emotion."

She felt a handwritten missive was much more satisfying . . . more like warm home cooking compared to an institutionalized meal.

One of my blog readers, Carrie, beautifully expressed this, *"I am doing a lot of writing of notes and cards to family and friends. It feeds my soul and lifts my spirit."* Yes, it does.

Ryder Carroll, the creator of the *Bullet Journal*, said, *"There's something incredibly powerful about making your mark on paper. It's the moment when an idea leaves your mind and looks back at you for the first time. I've never been able to replicate that experience digitally. It's not unlike Skyping with a close friend vs. having them over for dinner . . ."*

Early twentieth-century psychiatrist Karl Menninger was once asked what advice he would give a person who felt they were beginning to have a nervous breakdown. *"Lock up your house,"* he replied. *"Go across the railroad tracks, find someone in need, and do something* for him."

We help ourselves when we connect with others, and letter writing helps us to accomplish that.

The Intimacy of Writing

Notes and letters are so much more intimate than the other kinds of writing we do. The speeches of famous people help us understand their opinions and positions, but their correspondence gives us their humanity, their humor, and their truer personality. Their letters are more likely to shape our emotions about them. In *Newsweek*, Malcolm Jones summed it up well: *"Writing a lot of letters will not turn you into Lincoln or Shakespeare, but if you do it enough, you begin to put your essential self on paper whether you mean to or not. No other form of communication yet invented seems to encourage or support that revelatory intimacy."*

Blogger Rozanne Lopez speaks to this intimacy: *"Part of you comes through in your handwriting. I look back [on my writing] and without even reading the content, I can tell if I was stressed, sad, happy, grateful."*

When we write to others, we send a piece of ourselves.

The Sensory Pleasures

I once read a beautiful article in which the author spoke of writing on a desk that had belonged to both her mother and grandmother. She cherished every mark and groove in the well-worn wood, reflecting on the joys and sorrows shared, the tears shed, and the love expressed over the years in the notes and letters written there. That desk, for her, was alive with a spirit which permeated her own note-writing rituals and deepened her enjoyment of it. Perhaps you have such a desk or table to write on.

There is a strong tactile element to pouring your heartspoken thoughts onto a piece of paper. Columnist Steve Petrow describes one of its benefits: *"The tactile act of writing by hand allows me time to think before I commit to words; such a lost art can also be a deliberate way of feeling and remembering."*

I love picking out a card or choosing a particular stationery from the assortment I always have on hand to fit various situations or moods. Going into a store offering lovely papers and cards is a treat to the senses, and I'm unlikely to get out without a purchase. Smooth papers, textured papers, flecked papers, laid papers—they each offer a unique sensory feel to the note writer. Even the postage stamp can be a creative accessory adding visual appeal to the whole piece.

Scientists and graphic artists know the importance of color and its ability to create moods and even inspire action. Try livening up your writing life by having a few different colors of pen or bottled ink (for fountain pens) on hand. Choose a color to complement your stationery—or choose it to match your mood. Even ink color names contribute to my pleasure in writing with them: Serenity Blue, Red Dragon, Heart of Darkness, Irish Green.

Some of my more artistic friends cut out colorful images from magazines or add hand-drawn sketches to their notes. Others make their own paper and envelopes. When you add some of these touches, note writing can become a more enjoyable, even therapeutic, outlet for your creativity.

Have fun with it!

(See chapter VII: "Tools of the Trade" for more creative ideas.)

CHAPTER III
The Secret NOTES Formula

"Success has a simple formula: do your best and people may like it."

~ Sam Ewing

The Note in His Bible

Several years ago, my husband John, a retired physician, and I attended the funeral of a beloved pharmacist with whom John had enjoyed a long personal and professional friendship. As we waited to pay our respects to the family, his eldest daughter looked up and saw us. Breaking out of line, she hurried over and gave John a hug.

"Dr. Cottrell, Dad thought the world of you, and as we were going through his things, we found the letter you wrote him when he retired. It was in his Bible."

It was in his Bible!

Not only had he saved it, but he had kept it in a place most people reserve for their most precious papers. This letter made a difference to him, and in his absence, it gave his children a glimpse of the affection and respect felt by a local physician for their father's service to the community.

This is just one of many stories that contributed to my becoming such an ardent advocate for note writing. Time and again, I am struck by the power a simple note can possess—comfort in the most devastating and sad circumstances, not only to the note's receiver but also to those with whom they might share it.

Here are a few responses I've received after sending a personal note:

"As I read back over the many cards and notes I received when my mother died, I want to thank you for the lovely words you wrote about my mom."

"You have no idea how much your note meant to me and how comforting it was to know how much Stephen meant to you and others."

"When we were clearing out Daddy's things, there was a basket full of cards and letters he'd received during his illness, and so many of them were from you."

"We read your note to Daddy aloud while my siblings and spouses were all together with him. Please know you not only comforted him but the rest of us too. You clearly understood and appreciated Mother in such a special way."

"I know there's no etiquette requirement for writing a thank-you note to thank you for your thank-you note, but it warmed my heart so much, I had to let you know."

Nothing touches the heart and soul quite like a personal handwritten note that can be held, opened, read, and reread. The intimacy of holding the page touched by the sender—whose words were penned as an outpouring of love, gratitude, sympathy, or shared emotion—can only be matched by physically being with that person, holding their hand, and speaking to them in person. Most of us can point to a note or letter we received at the perfect time that felt like a hug or a healthy dose of love and support.

Before I get into the secret formula for writing notes, let me quickly address why some people feel writing them is a chore.

Why Does It Seem So Hard?

K nowing how meaningful personal notes can be to those we love, why do we find it so difficult to write them? Here are a few reasons, and some tips to help you overcome them:

- **We're busy and rushed.**

   True, but part of our job as stewards of our own time is to make space in our schedules for the most important actions, to prioritize those actions, and to make sure they align with our highest values. As a retiree with no children in the house, setting aside ten to fifteen minutes first thing in the morning—when I'm fresh—at least once a week ensures my most important notes get written. If you have young children or unusual work hours, try to identify other small pockets of time for this purpose.

- **We think writing notes takes a long time.**

   Most notes can be simple and short. I've scattered examples of lovely notes throughout this book. Using my secret NOTES formula will help you write a beautiful note quickly and easily every time. And, as with so many things, the more you do it, the easier it becomes.

🖋 **We think of it, but not at a convenient time to write.**

When it occurs to me that I should write a note—or if a friend or loved one crosses my mind as possibly needing encouragement or congratulations—I add it to my to-do list. Treat it the same way you would any other important task you don't want to forget. Use your Smartphone, iPad, or day planner. I sometimes leave myself a voicemail reminder message or send myself an email—whatever works for you.

🖋 **We think of it, but we don't have a pen and appropriate stationery close at hand.**

Keep attractive note cards, pen, and stamps in your purse, briefcase, or pocket. Turn those waiting times at the doctor's office or before a meeting into a note-writing opportunity. Create a writing space at home where your supplies—and a desk or lapboard—are ready when you are. (See chapter VII "Tools of the Trade" and my online resource page for links to wonderful note-writing accessories.)

🖋 **We procrastinate until it feels too late to send a note.**

It's rarely too late. In fact, in the case of sympathy notes, most people will tell you that notes and phone calls received later were especially appreciated because, after the initial outpouring of support, they soon felt alone in their grief while their friends kept going with their daily lives. And there is certainly never a deadline for gratitude or wishing someone well. The only mistake you can make is not reaching out at all.

🖋 **My hand hurts when I write.**

Some experience physical pain when they try to hold a pen or pencil. This might be from cramping, arthritis, or another inflammatory process. Happily, there are marvelous digital note-writing services available today, and their quality has improved tremendously over the last few years. I have tried a few, and they not only look like real handwriting, but they also use quality paper stock and are surprisingly affordable when you consider the cost of stationery, stamps, and time. Another option might be to dictate your message using speech-to-text software or apps. Then just print, fold, and mail. Many loving caretakers (or children, grandchildren, or friends) have experienced the joy of writing notes and letters dictated by someone unable to write themselves.

✒ We lack confidence we'll say the right thing.

This is the big one—the most common stumbling block to writing notes and letters—so if you recognized yourself here, you are not alone. Many, many people struggle over what to say, especially to someone who has suffered a terrible loss. I'll be giving lots of suggestions for this later, but don't let it stop you from writing. While I like to think my way with words is the secret ingredient to my effective note writing, I'll repeat what I said earlier: what most people remember is not the exact words. It's the fact they received a note from you and know you care—this is what stays with them.

Now, on to the secret NOTES formula . . .

The Secret NOTES
Formula Revealed

love acronyms, so as I began to consider the key elements in a heartspoken note, I thought an acronym might be a helpful memory hack, especially when you want a quick refresher on the principles I'm sharing. I use it myself.

Let **NOTES** be your easy-to-remember acronym for finding the right words for your heartspoken note, time and time again, regardless of the situation. You may not need every point for every note, but if you use this acronym like a checklist when you sit down to write, it will provide meaningful guidance.

N for Natural:

Write naturally, as though you are speaking in person. Flowery words are neither necessary nor effective. Think about what you would say to the person if they were sitting across the table from you and write with a personal touch. This warm, intimate style will serve you well.

Jane, I'm looking out the window at spring unfolding— remembering how we loved to look for the first bulbs

*to pop out of the ground and how grateful I am for our
lifelong friendship.*

*Susan, how I wish I could just reach out and give you a
great big hug.*

*Joan, what you're going through just stinks and I am
pounding on the gates of heaven for you to get some
relief.*

O for Open:

Before you start writing, take a few seconds to *open* your
heart and mind to inner guidance. Even if you're not traditionally
religious, this spiritual, meditative practice aligns you with the
person to whom you're writing and makes you more receptive
to thinking of what to say. Try to imagine where they are, what
they are going through, and what they might need to hear from
you. It is a time to be clear about your intention and trust your
heart's deep and innate wisdom. Once you've taken this short
reflective time, just start writing. You can always edit your words
later, but with practice, you won't need to.

T for Tell:

Don't beat around the bush; *tell* the person what you want
to say. If it's a sympathy note, it's okay to start by acknowledging
how inadequate words are, but you wanted to reach out to them
after the death of their loved one. If it's a thank-you note, tell
them how much you appreciate their gift or what they did for
you. If it's a congratulations note, tell them how pleased and
proud you are to learn of their accomplishment. You can often

use this "tell" sentence as the first line of your note. Sometimes the very best connection you can make with someone is simply to let him know you're sympathetic, proud, or grateful.

E for Empathize:

Empathize with the receiver, and in your mind's eye, put yourself in their situation and visualize them reading your note. Think about what your desired impact on them might be. Do you want to comfort or encourage them? Do you want them to know how much their deceased loved one meant to you? Do you want them to know how grateful you are or how proud? Do you simply want them to know they are remembered and appreciated? When you identify and feel what you want the outcome to be, the words will flow more easily.

> *Mary, words are so totally inadequate, but my heart is breaking for you and I just wanted you to know how much love is beaming your way.*

> *Jim, we got word about your recent promotion and just wanted you to know we are doing a happy dance to celebrate this well-deserved achievement.*

> *Uncle Joe, I don't know how you could have chosen a more perfect gift for my graduation than your father's pocket watch. I will treasure it always.*

S for Share:

Share a memory or experience. Be as specific as you can, considering your five senses as you choose your words. If you're writing a sympathy note, share a memory of the deceased or something you admired about them. Humorous memories can be comforting, even in times of loss.

> *I remember going fishing with Uncle Jim when I was a teenager, and he always made me feel so grown up. He loved the time I snagged an old shoe and thought I had the biggest fish in the lake.*

Be specific in other notes too. When you're thanking someone for a gift, share with them where you'll put it or how you'll use it. Details convey vividness and warmth and enable the giver to visualize you using their gift.

> *I was so excited to get your wonderful box of homemade cookies! With the stress of exams, I've been so homesick, and they were the perfect pick-me-up.*

> *Is there any more perfect combination than the delicious food and interesting conversation we enjoyed with you last weekend? What a lovely evening!*

There you have it. The secret's out. Learn this easy acronym and start using it to unleash your inner note writer. (See appendix B for this book's resource page URL and my secret NOTES formula download.)

What Should I Say?

"**W**hat should I say?" is the question I'm asked more than any other.

When I worry too much about whether I'll use exactly the right words, I always think of Carl W. Buehner's words (made famous by Maya Angelou): "*They may forget what you said—but they will never forget how you made them feel.*"

You'll find lots of samples for specific types of notes later in the book, but rather than try to remember particular words or phrases, I want to teach you some strategies for deriving personal, interesting, and unique content. Below are general writing techniques I've adapted for use in my personal correspondence.

✐ Use Stories

I used to think stories were only for fiction writers, but now I realize they enhance almost any kind of writing. In an exchange of letters—or even short notes—becoming a storyteller can make the most routine events more interesting, adding pleasure and readability. In a thank-you note, relate how you might use or enjoy the gift. In a sympathy note, share a vivid memory of the deceased. In a note of encouragement, express your own related experience or inspiration. Every note you write is a story, so make it a good one.

Use quotes

There are very few situations in which someone hasn't already had inspiring words to say, so if you're stuck for words, borrow a quote. Google is your friend here. Search for "Inspiring quotes about . . ." and fill in the blank (e.g., death, loss of spouse, loss of pet, congratulations, happy birthday, etc.). You will find many quotes to use or paraphrase.

Also enjoy my printable Heartspoken quote cards, which you can cut out and tuck into your notes. You may download these at no charge from the book's resource page on my website. (See appendix B for this URL and other downloadable checklists and printables.)

Grab some courage

When appropriate, don't be afraid to get vulnerable, take a stand, or voice an opinion. It will help make your note or letter more interesting and more likely to invite a response and subsequent conversation. I sometimes struggle with this myself, because I tend to avoid controversy and loathe the risk of hurting people's feelings. This tip doesn't always apply to more common correspondence, but if you're writing to convince someone of your position, be assertive. Remember to always—always—filter any assertiveness through your heart and choose your words with kindness. Ironically, this can be done even if you're angry, but it's not always easy.

Have a conversation

Though the person to whom you're writing isn't physically with you, it's still important to write as if they were; otherwise, it can sound like you're talking *at* them instead of *with* them.

Your imagination can be a secret weapon here. Visualize them sitting across the kitchen table from you with a cup of coffee or a glass of wine. What would you say to them? Imagine how your words might land if you were in their shoes.

When I'm reading a well-written note, I can see the other person in my mind's eye and hear their voice in my heart.

✎ Pretend you're in Hollywood

Okay, let's be honest. Sometimes you must thank someone for a gift you aren't truly thrilled about. Or you feel required to express sympathy for someone you don't know, or you never liked.

This is not the time for bluntness. Instead, without sacrificing your integrity, become an actor. A great actor doesn't just pretend to be the person he's playing; he becomes another person, channeling them and studying them until he becomes intimate with them. Then and only then can he render a convincing performance. You owe your friends, family, or clients the same degree of dedication to your craft. Here are some examples:

> *You were so thoughtful and generous to send us this antique pitcher. Just recently I was wishing for a pitcher when I realized I had nothing to put on the table for iced tea refills.* (They don't need to know you think it's ugly and heavy.)

> *I was touched and saddened to read Mark's obituary and realize how little I knew him and how wide-ranging his accomplishments were. He clearly made a difference in his time among us.* (They don't need to know Mark seemed rude and arrogant in your personal interactions with him.)

Twelve Note-Writing Tips:
A Checklist

While I've included the key tips to effective note writing in my secret NOTES formula, there are always more, so here's an expanded checklist for those who may find it more helpful than an acronym. Use it to polish your skills and get yourself unstuck if you don't know where to start or what to say. It will make note writing an enjoyable habit, and practice will give you confidence. (See appendix B for links to my resource page for this and other downloadable checklists and printables.)

☐ 1. **Make writing convenient.**

Keep a supply of quality notes and pens (and stamps and addresses) on hand. This way, when your inner voice whispers a name to your heart, you can write a note while it's on your mind. The biggest reason people write so few notes is procrastination and thinking someone would rather get a polished, carefully written note than a hastily written one. For most people, however, hearing from you is what counts, not the eloquence of your words.

☐ 2. **Be generous.**

Use any excuse to send someone a note to let them know you're thinking of them. Enclose an article you think would interest them or tell them about a book you've read or a movie you've seen. A terrific reason to write a personal note in business is when you can make a referral for someone else. They will be quicker to think about you and return the favor.

☐ 3. **Take a moment.**

Before you start writing, take a deep breath. Visualize the person receiving your note and hold them in your mind's eye. This makes them seem closer and allows you to focus on the things you wish to express to them.

☐ 4. **Write naturally.**

Keep your tone conversational, as though you were speaking to them in person. Be yourself. With few exceptions, personal notes are not the place for stiff, formal writing.

☐ 5. **Start by telling them why you're writing.**

You're thinking of them; you're missing them; you want to thank them; you want to congratulate them; you want to express sympathy or encouragement; you're grieving with them; you want to tell them about a resource you think they'll find helpful; you want to share surprise or joy over recent news. Whatever the reason, this is the place to start, and it usually primes the pump for what to say next.

☐ 6. **Be specific.**

Try to avoid, "Thank you for the lovely gift. I will enjoy using it." Instead, say, "The beautiful blue china teapot you gave me for my birthday makes me happy just looking at it. It reminds me of one my grandmother used to use. I'll think of you whenever I make tea in it!"

☐ 7. **Share stories and memories.**

It comforts someone grieving to know their loved one is remembered, especially when you can relate a happy memory or tell them of any way their loved one showed you a kindness or made an impact on your life. This tip can be equally meaningful in other kinds of notes:

Do you member the time we . . .?

I was driving through Virginia last week and happily remembered our crazy times swimming in Goose Creek.

Your father would be so proud of your promotion. I remember when he was about to pop over your Eagle Scout merit badge.

☐ 8. **Keep a log of your correspondence.**

Unless you have a terrific memory, you'll benefit from keeping a correspondence log. I used to use those little calendar/schedule books often given away by some companies. Today I use a small journal-style notebook which I keep near my stamps. Whenever I put a stamp on a letter, I log the date, the person to whom I'm writing, and a two-letter code for the purpose of the note (SY, sympathy, TY, thank you, CG, congratulations, etc. The full list of symbols I use and a journal page template can be found in chapter VII "Tools of the Trade"). Whether you use a log or a spreadsheet, make it simple and convenient so you'll use it.

☐ 9. **Think of your notes as hugs by mail.**

Through your words on paper, your heartspoken note is like wrapping your arms around someone to connect, comfort, encourage, or inspire. So, when words are hard to find, think about how you want your reader to feel when they read them. Tap into your heartfelt emotion to find the right words.

☐ **10. Short notes are fine.**

Two or three sentences can sometimes suffice in conveying your message, so don't be burdened by thinking you have to fill up a page with writing. My brother Bruce shared this delightful reflection on brevity:

> *"E. B. White was a master of the short communication. One of my favorite letters in a collection of his work ends with an apology to the recipient for the length of the letter. He said (paraphrasing Blaise Pascal), 'If I'd had more time, it would have been shorter.'"*

☐ **11. Proofread your note**

Look for spelling errors, overuse of certain words, or awkward sentences. If you're using a computer, don't rely on the spellcheck. I once caught a client's potentially embarrassing typo when she meant to write "public presentation" and left out the "l" in the first word. They were both correct in her spellchecker. If your note is handwritten, it's better to cross out a word and make the correction than to send it with unchecked errors.

☐ **12. Keep a "swipe file"**

The term "swipe file" refers to a collection of tested and proven words, sentences, or quotes you've loved enough to "swipe" from the author, write down, or record in a file or folder. They might be from books, podcasts, speeches, articles, or even cards and notes you've received yourself. Of course, you should always include in your notation where it came from so you can give credit to the author. This file can be a great source of ideas when you're searching for the right words for a particular note. I keep a special board in Trello for this, but Evernote or a Bullet Journal or a file folder work equally well.

In the end, it comes down to embracing the right mindset about personal note writing. Remember: it's not about how many notes we can send, but how many lives we can touch . . . how many hearts we can lighten . . . how many souls we can encourage. Start with whatever seems manageable to you, then nudge yourself to stick with it.

CHAPTER IV
A Note for Every Occasion

*"I keep all my letters, postcards, and thank-you notes.
I'll keep them forever!"*

~ Jane Levy

Thank You So Much

"Handwritten thank-you cards are the grace notes of life."

~ Marni Jameson

G ratitude is a powerful emotion. Studies from leading research centers consistently confirm an "attitude of gratitude" is beneficial on many levels: emotional, social, physical, career, and personality. In 2016, Dr. Erin Leyba reported in *Psychology Today* that researchers found those who are in the habit of expressing thanks tend to be happier, more positive, and more confident. This was true even after accounting for personality traits such as agreeableness and extraversion. Those who practice gratitude find it easier to cultivate meaningful friendships and relationships.

In so many circumstances, writing a personal note is one of the easiest and most effective ways to express your thanks and begin feeling those benefits of gratitude.

I confess I sometimes look at my "gifts received" list after Christmas with trepidation. So many thank-you notes to write! I've learned, though, to reframe this sense of obligation and turn it into one of joyful gratitude. Instead of thinking *I have to write these notes*, I tell myself, *I get to write these notes*. After all, someone thought of me and spent their money and time to purchase or make a gift they hoped I would enjoy. A thank-you note is such a small gesture of appreciation for kindness and generosity.

Why Write Thank-You Notes?

Let's go beyond what our mothers and grandmothers might have said if we asked them why we should write thank-you notes. "Because I said so" or "Because it's the right thing to do" are no longer enough to motivate most of us. There are many reasons beyond good manners and obligation to write expressions of gratitude.

✎ The Golden Rule

Of course, the golden rule comes to mind and certainly, good begets good and gratitude begets gratitude. It's a virtuous cycle. I am much more likely, for instance, to go out of my way to give a gift of time or treasure to someone who has been, in the past, grateful for my help, support, or generosity. My friend Katherine writes warm, lovely notes after being at our house for dinner, so she and her husband are always top of mind when we're thinking of someone to invite. When I hear of a young relative down on their luck, their past expression of authentic gratitude often triggers more generosity in me than I might otherwise feel. Every professional fundraiser knows this is true.

✎ The Gift

Your note itself is a gift of thoughtfulness. One of the most practical reasons for writing a thank-you note is to assure the giver their gift was, indeed, received, and it was what the giver intended. This is not only thoughtful but sometimes it's the chance to clear up a mistake.

I'll never forget writing my mother years ago to thank her for a lovely seashell centerpiece she had sent for my birthday. It seemed an odd gift for her to send since neither of us is particularly a "beach person," but who was I to question her taste? She called two days later. "That's not what I ordered at all!" she exclaimed. "It was supposed to be a vegetable bowl to match your plates." She corrected the order and made the exchange, but if I hadn't written her, that seashell centerpiece might still be gathering dust in the back of my closet.

The vagaries of postal service between the US and Great Britain make me extremely appreciative when my son and his wife write to let me know they have received gifts I've mailed. Packages are so easily stuck in customs or mistakenly delivered to a neighbor.

The Connection

Since the practice of sending notes—especially handwritten notes—is so rare today, your note will not only be noticed but will also be a lovely means of connection.

Without your note of thanks, the donor may have no idea how much their gift or action meant. This is your chance to go beyond the obligatory words and convey the true and full significance of what has been given to you. The secret to doing this is to be as specific as possible. Compare these two notes below. The first is all most people expect. The second imparts so much more:

> *"Thank you so much for the lovely blue dishes. We will enjoy using them."*

> *"We were thrilled to open your box and find these beautiful blue dishes. The color and style remind me so much of your kitchen and all the fabulous meals we've enjoyed there. They will go perfectly in our new home, and I'll think of you every time we use them. I can't wait to have our first party! It will feel as though you're right there with me."*

Paint a minds-eye picture for your gift giver so they can imagine you using their gift and derive pleasure from knowing you are truly going to enjoy it. My husband and I were touched by this heartwarming message received after sending a food tray to my friend Marty who had been sick. In this note, she not only painted that picture, she also strengthened our friendship and our anticipation of being together once she was feeling better:

> *"What a delightful gift we received from you two yesterday. We were so excited when it was delivered to the house. The variety of meats and cheeses was perfect. In fact, when we made our sandwiches, we each chose differently. The side dishes were yummy as well. Then there were the cinnamon buns to enjoy. Very delicious.*
>
> *"It has been a joy to know you as a couple and individually. We are blessed to have you in our lives. Have a lovely day and know your kindness will be feeding us for many days to come."*

The Benefit

Besides the proven health and relationship benefits of practicing a mindset of gratitude, there is also a related ripple effect. If I am thanked warmly for gifts given or kindness shown, I will not only be more likely to do it again for them, but I'm more likely to reach out to another person in a similar way. Appreciation and generosity are contagious. To be completely blunt here, donors are more likely to give you another gift later if you've thanked them for the one they've already given you. This is human nature.

A thank-you note is such a small token of appreciation. And we all love getting something besides bills in our mailbox. Every handwritten letter or note I receive is like getting love in the mail.

When Should I Send Thanks?

Let me count the times! Here are six to get you started, from the obvious to the more obscure:

1. For Gifts Received

Receiving a physical gift, of course, is the most classic reason and the most expected time to write a thank-you note. These gifts can accompany so many occasions: birthday, wedding, holiday, anniversary, retirement, going-away, housewarming.

All deserve a thank-you note, but length is not as important as sincerity. Be as specific as possible and try to share a detail about how the gift gave you pleasure or will be useful. Here's a wonderful example received from my nephew's wife, Kelly, after their wedding:

> *"Thank you so much for your amazing gift of a Cuisinart food processor! We are beyond excited to get started using it. Wells is especially excited to make huge batches of pesto and chimichurri! It will be such a great addition to our kitchen, and we will always think of you as we use it. We loved seeing you at the wedding and can't wait to get some more quality time soon. Thank you so much!"*

Some etiquette experts suggest it's not necessary to write a thank-you note for a gift given to you in person, because you would have already thanked the giver directly when it was received. I agree there is less urgency in this situation, but why not go beyond what you *should* do and consider what you *could* do?

2. For Hospitality Shown

These special occasions with friends and family can be memorable and soul-nourishing. And if you've ever hosted such a gathering, you know the preparation it takes, even when the menu is simple. Be sure to mention when your host or hostess has taken particular care in their culinary efforts, home décor, or other details that added to the event's pleasure. What was it you enjoyed the most about it? My friend Katherine is a master at writing thank-you notes that make us feel special and appreciated. I saved this recent one:

> *"What a comfort it was to enjoy that delicious dinner with good friends in your welcoming home. It has been a dark winter, and this was definitely a restorative moment. Thank you so much for having us and for your friendship."*

3. For a Listening Ear

A gift can be so much more than an object wrapped in paper and tied with a pretty bow. When someone gives you the gift of their time—to listen and perhaps offer feedback—their kindness deserves to be acknowledged with a personal note.

4. For Support or Encouragement

They might have shown up at your show, performance, or book signing. Perhaps they volunteered for your fundraising event. They might have called you before an important meeting or interview. They might have reminded you that you're perfect just the way you are (no matter what others say). The following is an excerpt from a note written by a young friend Linnea. She was thanking us for gifts, but she also included this lovely paragraph:

"I am so glad you could be at my wedding shower. You have been so impactful in my life, so I'm grateful I was able to celebrate with you. I appreciate not only the gifts but the expansive amount of help and support you have given me and my family over the years. I'm very thankful for you."

This is a note I've kept and cherished. A note like this lets someone know you noticed and appreciated their effort and thoughtfulness.

5. For Silent Companionship

Too often, our default way to comfort someone is trying to talk them into feeling better, to remind them things could be worse, or to gently chide them to "shake it off." Or perhaps we expect them to share the gory details of whatever is upsetting them.

More often, however, what we need when we're sad is someone to keep us company while we cry or rant or even sleep. If someone has shown up in your hour of need with no expectation except to keep you company, they have given you a precious gift of compassion and friendship. When you're able to muster the strength, let them know how grateful you are.

6. For Inspired Work

Have you ever finished an amazing book—or listened to an uplifting speech, or come to the end of a moving concert or theatrical performance—and realized your heart and mind were so full, you'll never be quite the same again? Why not write the creator and tell them? I've had lovely exchanges with authors, speakers, podcasters, and performers from doing this. Those who are not household names are grateful to know a stranger enjoyed their work. Even those with a wider following have been surprisingly gracious in their appreciation after I've written them. One example was Steve O'Keefe, author of *Set the Page on Fire: Secrets of Successful Writers*. After hearing about how much some of my writing friends and I liked his book, he offered to make an online visit to our writers' group to answer any questions.

Keep It Simple

We all put off writing personal notes from time to time. We convince ourselves they must be perfect, neat, and eloquent, so we have to be in the right mood, or we need a great deal of time. No! That is the devil on your shoulder talking, and this is one of those instances where "done is better than perfect."

Consider the lovely, simple thank-you note I received recently from a friend's daughter for a wedding shower gift I gave her:

> *"Thank you so much for the beautiful picture. I have never seen anything like it. We are planning to put it in our living room so we can see it every day. It is so lovely. Thank you!"*

It wasn't long and it wasn't fancy. It didn't need to be. It conveyed warmth and sincerity, and it made my day. Here's another note we received from our neighbor Teresa thanking us for our help during a family member's illness and subsequent death:

> *"Just a note to say thank you for always being there for us. How very fortunate and blessed we have been to have such wonderful neighbors."*

It's a nice touch when you can also express your appreciation for the sender as a person by mentioning something specific you admire or appreciate about them. "You always seem to know how to help," or "Your thoughtfulness means so very much" can go a long way.

Can You Say "Thank You" Too Often?

My dear friend Annette believes it's hard to thank someone too often. It's not that you should ever repeat the words "thank you" in short succession but rather that thanking someone for a gift given long ago can be especially meaningful. She recounted one example of thanking a family member for a robe not only immediately after receiving it but also several times over the years when she let them know she was still enjoying it and how it covered her with warmth and love every time she wore it. People do appreciate knowing when their gift has given repeated or long-lasting pleasure, enjoyment, or utility.

Help for the Overwhelmed Newlywed

I often hear from newlyweds that they feel almost paralyzed by the list of thank-you notes they need to write. When they can type faster than they can write, they often wish an email would suffice. It doesn't.

Sometimes I play tricks with myself to get through a mountain of notes to write. Since I've gotten so much pleasure out of *receiving* thank-you notes, I find I want to write them too. I know of no way through it except *through* it, but one way that has worked for me is to treat the task as I would a college reading assignment with a deadline. Choose a date by which you want to have your thank-you notes written and figure out how many to write per week—or into a daily goal if it's easier. Put it on your calendar in whatever increments work for you (one session per week, three shorter sessions, etc.). If you miss the mark one week, you know you've got to double up the next week.

Be realistic with yourself so you don't feel overwhelmed and write the most important notes first. Some couples split up the task, depending on who knew the gift-giver best. This not only lightened the load for both, but it ensured the notes were more personal.

If you're often on the go and find yourself with odd moments of waiting (for appointments, trains, etc.), you might find it helpful to put your list and your notecards, pen, stamps, etc., in a little tote bag and take it with you everywhere you go. This way, when you find a minute or two of waiting time, you can whip off one or two notes. (Make sure it's not the only copy of your list in case you misplace your tote bag.)

If you have a mobility or visual impairment, obviously people will cut you some slack. And options other than handwritten notes are available to you. It's so easy to record personal messages and email the audio or video file or put the recording file on a CD and mail it.

Phone calls, emails, and note-writing services to thank your gift givers are certainly better than nothing, but try to make them your absolute last resort. (See appendix D for such services.)

Whenever the devil on your shoulder starts whispering, "Oh, they don't really expect me to write a thank-you note" or "It's too much trouble when I have so many," remember the following:

- Whoever gave you the gift considered you enough to take the time to shop and spend their hard-earned money on something they thought you'd like. And late *is* better than never . . . even months late.

- If the gift giver ordered a gift to be sent to you, they may be anxious about whether you even received the gift.

- The time and energy you use to write a note is a gift itself. In these days of electronic communication, getting a handwritten note is like getting a hug by mail. Go ahead . . . make their day!

And yes, with few exceptions, they *do* expect you to write them a thank-you note. (See appendix B and D for more thank-you note resources.)

My Heart Is Broken: Expressing Sympathy

"This is not a good letter, Charlie. But I feel too sad to write a good one."

~ Ernest Hemingway

Death: Certain Yet Mysterious

In 1972, as a boy of fifteen, columnist Steven Petrow was so moved hearing about the loss of Senator Joe Biden's wife and infant daughter in a tragic accident, he wrote a note of sympathy and received a personal response. That note from Joe Biden, which Petrow has saved all these years, included these moving words: *"Now our life has been completely torn apart by an event I shall never completely understand."*

Forty-three years later, in 2015, Petrow found himself writing to Biden again, this time after learning about Biden's son Beau's untimely death from brain cancer. Reflecting on this later, Petrow made a poignant observation that underlies why it is so important to express our sympathy to those who have suffered a loss:

". . . Such a lost art [a handwritten note] can also be a deliberate way of feeling and remembering. Not because it's more 'proper' to hand-write a note than to use e-mail or post thoughts on social media, but because a death is so concrete

*and so permanent and so, too, should be the means of how
we express our loss."*

In a later article, he said when he sends a sympathy note, he hopes
it will provide *"a measure of indelible comfort in these dark times."* When
I read those words, I knew Mr. Petrow was a kindred spirit. When we
write notes of sympathy, we are offering *"indelible comfort."*

What to Say in a Comforting Sympathy Note

Next to thank-you notes, sympathy notes are perhaps the ones
we're called on to write the most often, yet for most of us, they are the
hardest to do. What do you say when you feel so helpless in the face
of someone else's loss? What good can your simple note do?

First, the act of writing is reaching out and providing a long-distance
embrace, regardless of the words you use. I often hear these notes are
saved and read later when they can be appreciated in a less emotional
time. So, get over your lack of confidence at knowing what to say and do
your best to convey your expression of love and shared loss. I appreciated
a friend's comment: *"For sure, writing to someone who is experiencing a
difficult time is a way to touch someone's heart."*

I take a moment before starting a sympathy note to visualize the
person, putting myself in their position, and trying to imagine what
might comfort me if I were in their place. This often helps me think
of what to say. It is completely okay to start with an honest statement:

> *Words are simply inadequate to express all that is on my heart
> after learning of Milton's death, but I had to let you know how
> much I'm thinking of you.*

Include specific happy memories of the deceased whenever possible, especially if they involve an event you shared or a good deed they did for you. These details can be powerful and comforting. My friend Anne shared this about notes she received after her father's death:

> "My father died when I was young. One note that was so precious to me was from another young person, a neighbor who also loved my dad. She wrote about how she'd always remember even the small things about my father, like how he could perch his glasses in the middle of his forehead when he wasn't using them, and how she marveled at the way he could read a paperback book and never crease the spine."

One of the devastating things about the loss of someone dear to you is the fear they will be forgotten, so for many, it is immensely comforting to hear their loved one's life validated in the stories of family and friends. If you don't have your own memories, you may have heard something worth sharing about the deceased. Let the person to whom you're writing know you believe the deceased person's life made a difference and he/she will be missed.

My friend Esther confirmed this with a fascinating insight into the importance of remembering and talking to survivors about those who have died:

> "I read many years ago that some Asian cultures have two different concepts of death. One is the death of the body; the other is the death of all the people who remember that person. As long as there is anyone alive who remembers them, they are not truly gone. I have often stated this in one way or another in sympathy notes.
>
> "A few years ago, I discovered how very true it is. I went to a reunion of the church I'd grown up in and so many people talked about my parents. There was even a woman there who

hadn't seen my mother since I was born, yet she told me how much my mother had influenced her formative years. Here was a total stranger to me, with so much of my mother still a living part of her!

"I find that such a comforting thought… those people who give themselves to other people continue to live on in those people long after their body has died. We need to share this with friends who are facing loss and let them know their loved one will live on as long as we are alive to remember them."

When you didn't know the deceased at all, you can still let the other person know you're holding them gently in your heart, lifting them up for healing, comfort, and peace. When we are in pain, it helps to know someone else understands. If you've been through a similar loss, it's tempting to share the experience so they will know you truly empathize. Be careful doing this—always remember it's about them, not about you. My writing friend Trudi shared a message she received and saved because it meant so much to her:

"May loving memories cradle you and new beginnings lead you."

Don't Forget to Connect Again Later

In the first few days and weeks after a death, family members are likely to get considerable emotional support and help from friends, family, and others in their community. My widow and widower friends have told me this support falls away quickly. The worst time for feeling lonely, they say, is later, after everyone has gone back to their normal lives and relatives have all gone home.

While it's always important to send a sympathy note right away, consider adding a reminder to your calendar to reach out in two or three months and again around the one-year anniversary of the death. I used to think this might bring more pain than consolation, but as I speak to friends who have lost loved ones, they tell me a note or phone call later is comforting not only for the kindness and connection but also for the reassurance their departed one is not forgotten.

Loss Comes in Many Shapes and Sizes

We think of sympathy notes after a death, but of course there are many other kinds of losses which might elicit your sympathy and a handwritten note:

- The loss of a job
- The loss of a business partner
- The loss of a relationship or marriage after a breakup or divorce

Throughout the COVID-19 pandemic, there have been so many unique kinds of losses—like milestone celebrations and traditional rites of passage: birthdays, college reunions, graduations, and weddings. I couldn't visit my mother in her retirement facility for several months. I have friends who were unable to be with their elderly parents when the parent was hospitalized, even dying. These are all variations of loss. Anyone would appreciate a heartfelt acknowledgement of what they're going through or have experienced.

The Loss of a Pet

I've had many questions specifically about what to say to someone who has lost a pet, so I am addressing it here. Even if you're not an "animal person," you probably have friends whose pets are like their children, and the loss of their pet can be absolutely devastating. You want to reach out but may find it hard to put your thoughts into words. Don't let this feeling of helplessness keep you from writing!

When my friend Pamela, one of the members of my Facebook

group, "The Art of the Heartspoken Note," lost her two adult cats and their new litter of kittens, other group members Beth, Jessica, and Andrea shared expressions of sympathy. I found these so moving:

"I am heartbroken for you! Losing any beloved furry family member is devastating. But let me assure you that, just like with human beings, the love we give and receive in return is so worth the pain of losing the beloved."

"Those fur babies went back to the God who loves them beyond measure, and who is so grateful you and your sweet husband loved them and cared for them with all your hearts."

"It takes great strength to love and care for vulnerable animals and people."

The following quotes expressing love and appreciation for animal companions may offer comfort to those who have lost beloved pets.

"Until one has loved an animal, a part of one's soul remains unawakened."

~ Anatole France

"The essential joy of being with horses is that it brings us in contact with the rare elements of grace, beauty, spirit, and freedom."

~ Sharon Ralls Lemon

"Not the least hard thing to bear when they go from us, these quiet friends, is that they carry away with them so many years of our own lives."

~ John Galsworthy

Other Quotes to Include in Sympathy Notes

Loss has been the subject of great writers and thinkers since the dawn of time, so when your own words don't seem enough or if you simply want to add a lovely touch, it's perfectly acceptable to borrow the words of others to express your sympathy. Always include proper accreditation. Here are a few:

> *"What we have once enjoyed and deeply loved we can never lose, for all that we love deeply becomes a part of us."*
>
> ~ Helen Keller

> *"Unable are the loved to die, for love is immortality."*
>
> ~ Emily Dickinson

> *"Those we love and lose are always connected by heartstrings into infinity."*
>
> ~ Terri Guillemets

> *"Like a bird singing in the rain, let grateful memories survive in time of sorrow."*
>
> ~ Robert Louis Stevenson

> *"What is lovely never dies, but passes into another loveliness, star-dust or sea-foam, flower or winged air."*
>
> ~ Thomas Bailey Aldrich

The scriptures of all the major religions include texts appropriate for comfort after loss, but these should be used only when you are sure of the receiver's faith preferences. You can find these by searching online for Christian, Muslim, or Buddhist sympathy quotes. I've included several in the book's resource page (See appendix C).

You can also add a lovely touch to any sympathy note with my Heartspoken Sympathy insert cards (see appendix B). Just print, cut them out, and tuck them in your card. With a lovely background image of mountains and sky, the card reads:

> *Our loved ones are beyond our sight,*
> *But they have not truly left us.*
> *We will feel their presence in*
> *the fragrant breath of spring,*
> *the healing warmth of summer,*
> *the exuberant brilliance of fall,*
> *and the exquisite clarity of winter.*
> *They live on whenever we pass to others*
> *the kindness they imparted*
> *the comfort they bestowed*
> *and the love they brought into our lives.*

Watch Out for These Sympathy-Note Landmines

- Avoid platitudes, religious or otherwise. It is not comforting to someone grieving, for instance, to be told God has a plan, even if you believe He does. And "God doesn't close doors without opening windows" may not land well in the immediate aftermath of a significant loss.

- Avoid using phrases that could seem like false comfort to someone who is grieving. For instance, a mother whose baby died does not want to hear she has plenty of time to have other children.

- Be careful not to minimize the loss with words such as, "You must be relieved that she is not suffering any longer" or "It's a blessing in disguise that he doesn't have to suffer anymore."

Though well-intentioned, these sentiments are not usually helpful immediately after a loss.

- Don't try to cheer people up. No one wants well-meaning encouragement to look on the bright side when their world has temporarily gone dark.

- It bears repeating: proofread carefully.

(See appendix B for links to my resource page for this and other downloadable checklists and printables.)

Way to Go! A Written Pat on The Back

"Congratulations aren't only given to praise someone's success . . . It's also a way of recognizing and supporting someone's happiness and good fortune."

~ Maggie Seaver

Life's milestones—graduations, engagements, retirements, promotions, awards, honors, achievements—are always sweeter when others participate in the celebrations or join in the chorus of those offering congratulations. While social media is a handy tool for conveying such sentiments, it can never replace those notes by mail.

My husband cherishes the many notes and cards he received when he retired from his medical practice, especially when they included a personal, handwritten message. After my dentist retired, he called to thank me for the note I had written him. He said it meant so much to hear from a patient who had appreciated his services.

I keep my Bullet Journal or paper (or electronic) to-do list close whenever I read the newspaper so I can jot down reminders to send notes when I see announcements or pictures. I'll often enclose newspaper clippings, and a note doesn't have to be long to be heartspoken. *"I'm so proud of you!"* or *"What an impressive achievement!"* or *"You are amazing!"* can be enough to make someone's day.

In his book *Stickin': The case for loyalty*, political strategist James

Carville shared this terrific advice: *"One of the lessons I learned [from my mother] is you can never tell anyone something too nice about their children."* Whenever you see or hear about the accomplishments of a young person you know, write to them *and* their parents.

Store-bought cards work well for a note of congratulations, but always include a personal note in addition to the printed message. Since I don't always have the right card on hand, I often use seasonal or colorful notecards that are blank inside to convey my short messages. Here are some examples:

- *"I was so happy to read about your promotion! We don't always get what we deserve in life, so I was glad to see you being recognized for your hard work and dedication."*

- *"Retirement! How happy I am for you and hope you find—as we have—that there's a whole new world of discovery and adventure awaiting."*

- *"How proud you must be of your daughter Susan's achievement on the basketball court [or as Valedictorian, or other achievement]! I thought you might enjoy having this clipping as a souvenir."*

- *"Graduation is such a wonderful accomplishment! It reflects your own dedication and hard work, and I wanted to congratulate you and wish you happiness and success in the days to come. I'm so proud of you."*

Hang in There: Words of Encouragement

"Be encouraged to be an encourager. It's a spiritual art that everyone can learn. And mostly you learn by practicing it."

~ Jill Briscoe

Encouragement can be so life-giving, especially when we feel the heavy weight of anxiety. No matter how upbeat we might be, everyone experiences down days, unexpected circumstances, unwanted diagnoses, accidents, failures, and even tragedies.

Whether these tough times are of our own making or just bad luck, these are the times when we need encouragement. And if we need it, so do others. Be alert for opportunities to offer a word of encouragement. Moments when one needs encouragement can be fleeting, so the timeliness of a response might mean it's perfectly okay for your loving comment to be delivered by a text message, a phone call, or even a private social media message. You may never know how much difference you'll make in someone's life.

Sending a note of encouragement is not about fixing a problem for someone. You usually can't. It's about letting them know they're not alone and you're thinking of them. It can also be pointing out good things they are unable to see in themselves, especially during dark times.

There is an amazing but little-known study by Dr. Jerome Motto from the early 1970s which shows irrefutable evidence that simple letters can, indeed, reduce the number of suicides. Those who have suffered from suicidal depression speak of feeling invisible, unseen, unwanted. A timely gesture of encouragement can sometimes break such downward spirals of negative thinking and create enough light for the person to see their way to a happier state of mind.

Don't Believe the "Black Hole" Lie

Maybe you've reached out to someone in the past—written a note . . . left a message . . . sent a gift—but got no response at all.

Crickets—nada—nothing.

Getting no response from our notes of encouragement doesn't mean we shouldn't keep writing them. Yes, it's tempting to believe it's too much trouble to write a note or make a phone call when we don't know if it helped or not.

Do it anyway.

Don't wait for an obvious sign or a tragedy to happen. Adopt an ongoing mindset of encouragement and let your friends and family know you're thinking of them and that they matter to you. We can't reach everyone who needs it, but any kindness we do—no matter how small—has the potential to make a difference. You've probably been on the receiving end of such a kindness, so you know it to be true.

We who love to write notes and letters have such a powerful way to convey kindness—and it's right at our fingertips. If you're thinking of someone right now, put this book down and write them a note.

Encouraging Young People

One fateful summer of childhood, when I was eleven years old, I thought I wanted to go to camp, but I had no idea how wrong I was. I've never been so homesick in my life (and I never went back). But oh, those letters from my family helped! They were like lifelines keeping me afloat until I could go home again.

When I was in high school, I was a five-day boarder, but even coming home every weekend, I experienced homesickness. I never missed a daily trip to the mailbox to see if I'd received any mail. I was happier in college, but the joy of receiving personal mail still comes back to me to this day.

So, if you know a young person who's away at school or a job for the first time, consider brightening their day with a bit of snail mail. I still have wonderful letters from my parents and grandparents, filled with precious memories and great wisdom.

Don't ever underestimate how much a simple handwritten note will mean to someone of any age. I sent this letter to a high school senior friend who had recently gotten into the college of his choice. His mother told me he read it to her on the phone and loved getting it.

> *"I wanted to write and tell you how proud Dr. John and I are of you in getting accepted to Penn State. We were already proud of you, regardless of whether Penn State had the good sense to accept you or not. You've worked hard, you've tried a lot of interesting things, and you've been involved in the life of your school and your community. These will all equip you well for whatever lies ahead, and we can't wait to see what that will be! And always remember this: whenever you stumble, you certainly haven't failed. You've just learned how NOT to do something the next time. Playing it safe in life has far fewer mistakes, but far fewer adventures."*

My niece Eliza's first week at college coincided with her birthday, so I decided to write her a letter instead of just sending a card. It made my day to see her Facebook page a few days later with her post, *"I just got a letter! I just got a letter!"*

I asked my blog readers to share stories of receiving mail when they were away from home. Here are some of their heartwarming responses:

"When we first moved away from home, my dad used to send my son letters all the time. It was always exciting for him to know his Papa hadn't forgot him even though we didn't live there anymore."

~ Helena

"The day after graduating high school, my upside-down family situation had me moving away from my hometown. It was sad and yet exciting, but the most marvelous thing was that over the next several years I received an abundance of letters from friends from home. Even those who hadn't especially been my 'nearest and dearest' over the course of growing up together in a small town became my 'nearest and dearest' through their uplifting and thoughtful letters. Those letters were, and remain, much treasured."

~ Barbara

"Did I ever receive a letter that lifted my spirits when I was away from home? Oh yeah! Every Tuesday. I was only thirty miles from home, but it might as well have been 3,000. My mother wrote to me a little bit every day. On Monday she would mail the letter and start a new one. Every Tuesday I had a chronicle of the past week at home. Mother died before I finished college. Her letters, in her beautiful, award-winning handwriting, bring her back to me as nothing else can."

~ Esther

It's so easy! Get out your pen and paper and write. And if you must, call a young person's parents to get their mailing address; you'll make their day too. Of course, you'll get extra points if you tuck the note into a box of homemade cookies.

Messages of Encouragement

- Please know I'm thinking of you today and hope you can feel the loving energy from those who love and care about you.

- You are loved and thought of today. Have a great week!

- I'm sending you warm thoughts during this difficult time. I hope things will feel more hopeful very soon. Hang in there.

- I know your heart is heavy. I understand and would love to lighten your load if I can.

- I know you, and you are much stronger than you may think— keep your head up, eyes forward, and with one step at a time, you'll get to a better place.

- No matter where I go and no matter what I do, you will ride lightly on my heart, and I will be saying prayers for your well-being and happiness.

- You have been with me in some of the darkest times of my life. I want to do the same for you.

- You are not alone—I will walk beside you and we'll get through this together.

- You are loved, seen, and so important to those of us who care about you.

Short and sweet can sometimes be best:

- I love you!

- You are a wonderful parent!

- Have a good day!

- Thank you for being such a dear friend to me!

- This verse reminded me of you . . .

I love what motivational speaker John C. Maxwell says about being an encourager:

> *"Everyone has the potential to become an encourager. You don't have to be rich. You don't have to be a genius. You don't have to have it all together. All you have to do is care about people and initiate."*

Amen to that.

I Hate That You're Sick!
Get-Well Notes

"The best of healers is good cheer."

~ Pindus

Get-well cards and notes are among the most sent, as evidenced by the shelf space allotted to them in stores. While I often use colorful, happy-themed notecards with blank insides, I am always on the lookout for reasonably priced, cheerful get-well cards (your local Dollar Stores are often great places to do this). I like having them on hand when I need them, and psychologically, it seems easier to grab a card with a good message already in it, but always add a personal note in addition to the card's message.

Nothing's ever simple, and a standard get-well card or note may not always be appropriate for anyone who is ill. When choosing the right card or heartspoken words for a note to someone sick, it's important to consider what kind of illness they are experiencing. That usually falls in one of three categories:

- **Short-term conditions** from which they are expected to recover quickly such as the flu or a cold, surgery, or an injury that will heal.

- **Chronic illness** such as severe arthritis, heart condition, or anything they are likely to be dealing with for a long time or for the rest of their life.

- **Terminal illness** when they are not expected to recover.

Short-term maladies are well-suited for the traditional get-well card or note, and a touch of humor can be especially cheerful. Your card delivers a hug when you can't do it in person.

Chronic illness calls for an entirely different kind of message—one with more encouragement. It recognizes that someone is dealing with a condition unlikely to resolve completely. Your goal is to try to lift them up and let them know you're thinking of them. You want them to know you hate what they're going through. Their condition is long-term, so consider dropping them a line every so often.

Writing to someone with a terminal diagnosis is one of the hardest notes to write—how can you comfort someone who's been given what they might well consider a death sentence? It's okay to say, *"This really stinks"* or "I'm shaking my fist at Heaven over this." But avoid platitudes and sappy sentiment. Speak from your heart. *"Call me if there's anything I can do"* is too vague to be very helpful. In her wonderful memoir, cancer survivor Kate Bowler said she usually didn't want to talk about her illness, and instead, *". . . sometimes I want a hug and a recap of American Ninja Warrior."*

In place of an indefinite offer to help, be as specific as possible so they'll be more likely to take you up on it. Questions like *"May I bring supper next Tuesday?"* or *"May I get you anything when I go to the grocery on Friday?"* or *"May I pick up the kids after soccer practice for you?"* are direct ways to help. Organizing a series of meals to be delivered over a period of time is almost always welcome, but call first to inquire about food allergies/preferences and find out a convenient time for delivery.

I'm So Sorry: Notes
of Apology

"A meaningful apology is one that communicates three Rs: regret, responsibility, and remedy."

~ Beverly Engel

S adly, not one of us is perfect. We have all made mistakes and have hurt or offended others, even if we didn't mean to. As hard as it is to do, a genuine apology is often the most direct and effective way to diffuse the situation and move toward restoring a damaged relationship.

Timing and knowing the offended party are both key elements in a meaningful apology. While a face-to-face meeting is often best, sometimes a note of apology can be appropriate and easier on you both. Whole books have been written on the subject (Dr. Harriet Lerner's excellent book on this is included in the bibliography), but any effective apology should include an acknowledgment of your error, an explanation that takes responsibility, an expression of sincere regret, and an attempt to make things right between you.

Why is it so hard to apologize? The answer is probably a combination of factors:

- It's human to be defensive, and the feeling of shame is one most of us try to avoid.

- We equate making a mistake with being a bad person.

- We might think admitting a mistake will make us more vulnerable to additional criticism.

- We're afraid an apology won't help.

- Often, it's not all our fault, so we're reluctant to imply it is.

Do your best to move past the defensiveness. What we *do* is not who we *are*, and while an apology might open us up to more criticism, it more often results in a reset and an opportunity for everyone to shift gears. An apology won't always help, but it might do more good than you can imagine.

You don't have to accept all the blame if it isn't all your fault; you can limit your apology to what you might have been responsible for. Your apology may inspire the other person to acknowledge their own role in the problem.

When we send a written apology, we at least have time to think about what we want to say and craft our best response to the situation. Take the time to quiet yourself and listen to your heart for the right words. As always, try to focus on the other person instead of yourself. Here are the key elements to include:

- Just say, *"I'm sorry"* and don't put a "but" after it. When you add a condition—or suggest you're not the only one at fault—you dilute your apology and risk putting them on the defensive. It comes across as sounding like you're insincere and only going through the motions.

- Take responsibility for what happened or for your part in it. *"I wish I could take it back. I clearly didn't consider your feelings."*

- Articulate what happened so the other person knows you understand and why you feel the need to apologize. Address your role and resist passing the blame onto someone else.

- State how you plan to make the situation better. Sometimes it's appropriate to ask the other person how you can make amends.

- Ask for forgiveness.

As a former officer of a nonprofit, here is a note I wrote to a donor whose check went undeposited for too long.

> *"Your concerns and your constructive criticism are fair and valid, and I am very embarrassed about it. This has never happened before and I can assure you, it won't happen again. Since your email, we have had a serious dialogue about our internal procedures to ensure it does not, so despite our chagrin, we are grateful for your communication and the opportunity to fix something that needed fixing.*
>
> *"We work hard to get things right and we clearly missed the mark on this one. There are reasons it happened, but no excuses. Please know how seriously we have taken this issue and give us another chance to regain your confidence."*

A note of apology calls on many of the characteristics we strive to cultivate in the heartspoken life: empathy, kindness, courage, and love. These will serve as beacons to guide you on your path.

I Forgive You

"If we really want to love, we must learn how to forgive."

~ Mother Theresa

On the flip side of apology is forgiveness. Perhaps you have received a request for pardon from someone who has hurt or offended you. Carrying unresolved anger and resentment ultimately hurts us more than the person who caused it, but still, it can be so hard to forgive them, forego revenge, and let go of bitterness. Give yourself time to work through your emotions; then you will hopefully be able to offer the absolution they seek. In time, you will find more peace too.

In a note of forgiveness, empathy can again come to your rescue as you consider how the other person might feel. As St. Augustine first suggested—and many have said since—try to "hate the sin but love the sinner." Forgiving someone does not mean you're forgetting or condoning what was done, and it certainly doesn't mean you're weak. It does mean you're canceling a debt and offering the person who hurt you a gift, whether it is deserved or not.

A sincere note from your heart will break the invisible chains that enslave you both. At the least, it can clear the air; at best, it can restore your relationship.

Holiday Notes:
A Few Pointers

"Receiving a handwritten note or card has a far greater emotional impact and makes people feel far more special and cared about than receiving emails or texts."

~ Mindlab research study for the Royal Mail

Embrace the Spirit of the Season

Whatever your faith and its traditions, your priority during any holiday season is to remember why and what you are celebrating. Embrace the season by practicing and enjoying its meaningful traditions with family and loved ones. Sending holiday cards—for me, that means Christmas cards—is often one of those traditions, but it also might seem like the last thing you need during a time when you already feel overwhelmed.

While self-care and common sense must be considered, when I harness the spirit of spreading love, joy, and peace, I enjoy writing and sending cards more. That spirit will hopefully infuse my messages and be felt when they open and read my card.

In an article for *The Washington Post*, Georgia Lewis wrote about her lifetime of holiday cards sent and received and the simple things conveyed in those cards. *"Those simple things,"* she wrote, *"are, of course, the things that count the most."* The early years were filled with recent marriages, new babies, and news about careers. Ensuing years brought notes about divorces, empty nests, aging parents, and grandchildren. Before long, the news was more bittersweet as friends died or moved to nursing homes. But the author cherished them all in the article's lovely title: *"Christmas cards stitch up the threads of a lifetime."* Indeed, they do.

Here's What I Do to Make Holiday Card Writing More Manageable:

I start by creating a card station in a corner of my home in early December with boxes of cards, stamps, pens, holiday-themed postage stamps, return address labels, and my list of names and addresses—everything I need. When I receive cards, I check the return address to update my records. I create a fresh checklist every year so I can keep track of sent and received cards.

About the third week of December, I usually get behind in responding to those who have sent us a card, but I try hard not to let it create stress. A card sent before the end of the twelve days of Christmas (January 6) is a Christmas card. One sent later in January is a New Year's card. If it's sent after January, I shift gears to my next suggestion.

Divide and Conquer

Who says all your once-a-year card recipients need to hear from you in December? Instead of sending fifty Christmas cards, for instance, consider making several of them Thanksgiving cards to mail in November or New Year's cards which can be sent any time in January. Or divide your list of names further into twelve parts and touch bases with a few each month instead of all of them in a much shorter timeframe. Some friends might wonder why they haven't heard from you, but when they get a longer and more personal note from you later in the year, they'll enjoy it more than a hurried note in December.

If you feel the need to link your notes to a holiday, there are many throughout the year. (See appendix B for a monthly list of holidays.)

Whenever you decide to send notes, resist the urge to rush. Remember the Heartspoken way is all about connection, and it only takes a moment to visualize the other person and send loving energy along with your message. We all enjoy a card with a personal message so much, even if it's written at the top or bottom of a generic holiday letter or card.

Don't Let These Situations Trip You Up

As you peruse your list, you may wince when you see names you've neglected for a while. If it's important to you to let them know you're thinking of them, do it. (If it's not, don't include them on your next list. It's perfectly natural to lose touch with a few people as your life changes.) An honest sentiment like, *"I think of you way more than you'll ever know"* or *"The miles between us are no excuse for my being out of touch for so long. Please know I'm thinking of you."*

It's okay to acknowledge a recent loss or a hard year for the person to whom you're writing. Sugarcoating difficult circumstances often feels false to the receiver. Consider phrases like *"I hate that you've had such a rough year"* or *"I am holding you and your family close in my thoughts"* or *"Take care of yourself—you deserve it"* or *"I wish Tom was still with us, but we hold him in our hearts."*

On the flip side, you may have had your own bad year. If a death has derailed you emotionally, for instance, you may need to skip a year of sending holiday cards. Be kind to yourself, if you can, but consider those on your list who might particularly want to know what has happened so they can support you.

Note Starters

If you need a phrase to prime the pump of your note-writing flow, consider these:

- This time of year always reminds me of . . .
- As I count my blessings this time of year, your friendship is high on the list . . .
- Do you know what I miss the most?
- This past year, we decided to . . .
- I'm still enjoying the warm blanket you gave me . . .
- You should see . . .
- Remember the time when . . .

Try to make the writing of notes and cards an act of love, not of obligation. It will make all the difference to the reader when they receive it.

Who Needs an Excuse?

"You'll make someone happy. The receiver of your letter is going to get a burst of excitement and know that you care. This, in turn, will make you feel good about yourself."

~ MiNDFOOD #SmartThinking website

A ny time is a good time to let someone know you're thinking of them. There might be a trigger date on the calendar or no reason at all. Totally unexpected notes have been among the nicest I've ever received. Here are a few ideas to begin your note:

- I thought of you when I saw _____, read _____, heard _____, etc. . . .

- I just wanted to send a hug by mail . . .

- This time of year always reminds me of our summer at the beach . . .

- I've been a poor correspondent, but I think of you so often . . .

- Veterans Day made me think of you and want to express my heartfelt thanks for your service to our country.

- It's your birthday! I hope you're doing something fun to celebrate!

> I've been thinking about the conversation we couldn't finish when we were together at Easter. It was wonderful to talk, but there's never enough time!

Sometimes, the still, small voice urging you to reach out to someone may get louder and feel more serious. Maybe you write, *"You've come to mind several times since I woke up this morning, so I wanted to make sure you're okay."* This sense of urgency might also call for a more immediate contact by phone or email.

My dear friend Karen is good at picking up vibes from me when I'm sad or stressed. Her note (or email or phone call) might be an expression of support, a pick-me-up joke, a prayer, or an inspiring quote. This has taught me to pay more attention when someone comes to mind for no known reason, especially if they are someone I don't see very often. "The Great Pause" of COVID-19 has included many such instances.

You don't need to have a special reason to write a heartspoken note, and it doesn't have to be long. That same friend, Karen, sent a note recently that said, *"Elizabeth, my life is rich because of you. Blessings to you and John."* If you think of someone, let them know.

CHAPTER V
Outside-the-Box Note Writing

"Sometimes, reaching out and taking someone's hand is the beginning of a journey. At other times it is allowing another to take yours."

~ Vera Nazarian

Ministries and Causes

Perhaps you feel a spiritual call to note writing that goes far beyond common obligation or etiquette. I do, and I believe it has to do with the practice of reaching out to others being a form of love in action—the foundation for all the major faith traditions. Note writing is one manifestation of this love, and it can be so profound because it strengthens our connection with others. I am reminded of this verse from Holy Scripture, in Proverbs 12:25 (NRSV): *"Anxiety weighs down the human heart, but a good word cheers it up."*

We can all be part of our own encouragement ministry. Here are some wonderful things to say:

- You are not alone. I'm rooting for you.

- You are loved, seen, and so important.

- Thank you for being such a dear friend.

- You are an amazing parent.

- I love you!

- What you're going through is really tough. I'm here if you need me.

My friends Barb and Ann have made note writing a true ministry. Their fortunate family, friends, and acquaintances are likely to have notes from them recognizing life's various milestones and events: births and deaths, birthdays and anniversaries, promotions, and retirements. I try to emulate their faithfulness, because we all believe sending a heartspoken note is sharing God's love by mail.

I once worked with a group called Noteworthy Thoughts founded by a high school classmate of mine. They describe themselves as a "community initiative to recognize good deeds and to build bridges of human connection." Some of my notes went to politicians or other public figures who had exhibited courage or stamina by taking unpopular stands. Others went to elementary school children whose schoolmates had been victims of recent school shootings.

During the COVID pandemic, members of my Facebook group "The Art of the Heartspoken Note" shared many examples of pop-up note-writing projects to thank and encourage healthcare workers and emergency personnel or to reach out to nursing home residents who were on lockdown and unable to receive visits from family and friends.

There are many similar charitable organizations whose mission is to organize letter-writing campaigns to various groups such as active-duty soldiers, school children, nursing home residents, medical care center residents, cancer patients, wounded veterans, and more. If writing letters to help someone in need sounds appealing, search the internet for "letter-writing charities."

Of course, you don't need to belong to a group to engage in this sort of spiritual outreach. Every day the news is filled with stories of individuals who could use a heartspoken word of cheer or support. Simply take out your pen and paper and write.

When you support a cause, you become part of the solution, so consider how your note writing could benefit a charity you believe in.

Nonprofit organizations thrive on the stories they receive from anyone who has benefitted from their work or who can affirm its value. Charitable work sometimes feels thankless. By taking the time to support a cause or benevolent organization, to let them know they are making a difference, you often help reignite their hope and dedication.

You may choose to write to specific individuals you find who are working in the area you wish to support, or you may look up the officers of a nonprofit organization and send a note to the executive director or the chairman of the board. I am sometimes reminded to write this kind of note after reading about an award given or a grant received by one of my favorite causes.

Politics offer an entirely different opportunity for note writing, especially with undecided or unregistered voters. Studies show that receiving a handwritten postcard after receiving a voter registration form increased the likelihood of returning the form by 20 percent. I have also written notes to local candidates thanking them for stepping up to run for public office.

Fan Mail

Have you ever read a book or article, watched a movie, or listened to a musical performance or podcast that left you feeling profoundly moved by the virtuosity of its creator or performer? Perhaps its message inspired you to take action or changed forever the way you perceived an issue. Creators need to hear when their work has touched their audience so they can be inspired to keep creating. What better way to let them know how you feel and how their work impacted you than through a heartspoken, handwritten note?

Yes, famous individuals—especially movie stars—are likely to be overwhelmed by fan mail and may never personally read your missive (but you never know). However, thousands of other creators toil in virtual solitude. They pour their heart and soul into their work and offer it to the world, often wondering if it has disappeared into a black hole. A personal note could mean so much to them, and you may even get a personal reply.

One memorable response I received came from writer and activist Parker J. Palmer, who thanked me warmly for my comments to him about his then-new podcast "The Growing Edge" that he and Carrie Newcomer were producing. He even asked if he might use them as a testimonial.

Another was from Pulitzer prize-winning journalist Connie Schultz, whose columns during the pandemic were often soul-nourishing to me. She responded to my note of appreciation with a lovely, warm, handwritten reply saying how glad she was to have a friend in the Shenandoah Valley.

New York Times best-selling author Jason F. Wright, to whom I'd written to thank him for his books and inspirational articles in our local paper, expressed appreciation for my support of him and his family in a personal video message. And then he graciously agreed to write the foreword to this book!

Everyone is concerned today about protecting our privacy, so it's not surprising that the biggest stumbling block in writing fan mail is the challenge of finding their postal address. The less famous the person is, the easier it is to find their address. Sometimes a mailing address can be found in their book, on their website, or on a social media profile. Since many publishers and agents serve as gatekeepers to protect their clients, I have had some success in writing to an author's publisher and asking them to forward my note. My subscription to WhitePages.com can occasionally offer a solution if I know what town they live in, but it may take a bit of sleuthing. My fallback is to scan my handwritten note and attach the digital file in an email or social media message to them.

You may not get a response. You will rarely ever learn if your notes are seen. But you have supported quality work and enjoyed the positive feelings resulting from genuine expressions of gratitude and appreciation.

A Wedding Gift to the Bride and Groom's Parents

Lynette M. Smith, author of *How to Write Heartfelt Letters to Treasure: For Special Occasions and Occasions Made Special,* gave me permission to share this wonderful family story about an unusual use of personal letters:

"When our son Byron married Rachael on November 22, 2008, instead of buying gifts for their parents to commemorate the occasion, they created lasting memories that touched our hearts. They each wrote a loving letter to their own parents, describing not only their fondest childhood memories but also the values, life lessons, and ideals they would bring to their marriage.

"At the wedding rehearsal dinner, the two of them formally presented these beautifully framed letters to my husband me, and to Rachael's parents. Everyone was deeply moved when the best man and maid of honor read the letters aloud as Byron and Rachael stood beside their parents. Even today, when I read our son's letter, I feel just as moved as when it was first presented. My husband and I display our letter in a place of honor in our home, and we will always treasure this loving memento from our son—it has been so much more meaningful than a purchased gift ever could have been."

Notes to Strangers

W hen I first moved to Shenandoah County and became involved in civic activities, I received several lovely notes from a wonderful woman named Florence Young. A member of the Shenandoah County School Board, Florence wrote hundreds of encouraging notes to young men and women, many of whom she'd never met. Every time I write a note of support, sympathy, or encouragement to a stranger, I think of her and remember how her notes made me feel seen and appreciated.

In the spirit of "random acts of kindness," Hannah Brencher recounts, in her popular TED Talk, how she fought through her own depression by leaving anonymous love letters in public places.

London artist Andy Leek found a similar outlet for his creativity and desire to make others happy. He left random messages on the seats and benches of commuter trains.

Creative entrepreneur Laura West's #JoySpark cards are inspirational notes on colorful paper expressing love and encouragement. Again, they are left for strangers in public places: with your tip at a restaurant, in a bag with a customer's purchase, on the table at a doctor's office. *"When you spend a bit of time making a personal card (even a very simple one) and then give it to someone,"* says West, *"you are giving your energy,*

creativity, and joy. And . . . you get back huge waves of feel-good vibes."
I loved this idea from my friend Karen in North Dakota:

> "Over the last two Covid years, when I have a bank deposit to make, I always mail it. I put the deposit slip and check inside one of my personal art cards. I also include a brief message. From a simple 'Thank you for handling my deposit today!' to messages like 'Are you sick of winter? I sure am. Spring is coming!' or 'I saw the geese coming in today—that means spring is just around the corner.' I got a handwritten note today from the local client relationship consultant thanking me for the cards I send with my deposits. Heartspoken notes are appreciated."

I saw on a recent TV spot that New York City resident Coretta James has written thousands of thank-you notes to New York Police Department officers, with a goal of writing to each one of the 36,000 officers in the department. She wanted to counter the negative attitude toward police that is causing a spike in retirements and causing low morale. She is reminding them that they're special and they're appreciated for putting their lives on the line every single day. Any law enforcement officer would appreciate that kind of note.

In a heartwarming article for *The Washington Post*, journalist Sydney Page shared the story of Deshauna Priest who, as part of a third-grade class project, wrote a heartspoken note to a World War II veteran she did not know. Its message was simply, *"Thank you for saving us from Hitler. If it wasn't for you, we would never have freedom. You made freedom for us. You sacrificed your own life."* The veteran, Frank Grasberger, was moved to tears to receive such a stirring message from someone so young, and he wrote back in care of her school, not knowing if she had received it. He carried that letter with him for the next twelve years, trying hard to find the young woman to thank her. Intrigued by the challenge of connecting the two, the resident services director of his retirement home joined the search and was able to bring them together for a tearful reunion. By then, Deshauna was, herself, in the National Guard, and she arrived for the reunion in her uniform with a bouquet of roses for the ninety-five-year-old Grasberger.

Another wonderful story came from an Alabama TV station about an elderly WWII vet, George Mills, who, for his one-hundredth birthday, received notes of gratitude from many Germans, including one from Angela Merkel, the Chancellor of Germany at the time. The note-writing effort was spearheaded by a German named Tobias who Mills met when he returned to Germany seventy-five years after the war to visit some of the places where he had fought and the place he was taken prisoner. Tobias explained that the Allies had saved them from the tyranny of Hitler, and they wanted Mills to know how thankful they were for his part in liberating them.

Corresponding with Children

Sadly, writing notes, especially thank you notes, is not something that comes naturally to most children, especially if they don't see their parents writing notes. They need to be taught and encouraged (maybe nudged strongly) from an early age not only to learn how to do it but also when to do it. For years, I made each of my children a list of their gifts after Christmas and birthdays, complete with the stationery, stamps, and the names and addresses of those who needed to be thanked. It worked best when I sat down to write my own notes while they were writing theirs. I didn't ask to read the notes, but I did—at least for a while—have "show and tell" to make sure they were written. Early on, I talked to them about what to say, but I resisted the temptation to correct their missives so as not to make them feel judged and defensive. I wanted them to look forward to their next writing session with me.

My husband and I once received a delightful note from three very young siblings whose grandparents brought them over for a summer swim. The oldest penned the note and all three signed it. This smart grandmother knew a teachable moment when she saw it, and we loved getting the note from the children themselves.

Grandparents often write me to ask how I would encourage young children or grandchildren to write more notes. Of course, writing to them is wonderful encouragement so they can experience the joy of receiving a note or letter in the mail. I still have a stash of letters from my own grandfather in which he told me about his activities and interests and expressed pride in my achievements and good grades. He almost always included a bit of sage advice or wisdom. I loved hearing about his fishing trips, his daily routines with Grandmother, and his opinions about what was going on in the world.

Young children often feel more grown-up when they're encouraged to write a note, even when the recipient may not have a clue what the child is saying. My friend Lois recalls receiving a video of her four-year-old granddaughter "writing a letter to Grandma." The child was being interviewed by her mother about what she was writing. *"What a treasure this was!"* Lois recalls.

Some children are motivated when you give them their own personalized stationery, perhaps accompanied by some interesting postage stamps and colored pens—maybe even some age-appropriate stickers. International etiquette expert Lydia Ramsey sent me a picture of a cherished and adorable handwritten note she received from her twelve-year-old grandson, written on a personalized notecard. It said, *"Dear Mutti, Thank you for the Smart Plug. I will use it a lot for whatever I use it for. Love, Aiden."*

Young children can start by using templates. I've created two that you can download from my book resource page (https://heartspoken. com/heartspoken-book-resources).

My friend Karen shared a wonderful idea about motivating a young person's interest by writing in code:

> *"In the late nineties, my son attended a military academy in Pennsylvania for his junior and senior years of high school. I lived in Delaware, so we wrote letters. He created a 'secret code' for fun. In one letter, he sent me the key showing a different character for each letter of the alphabet. The characters*

were all made up—loops and weird jagged lines and circles in circles and upside-down Vs and upside-down Ts and dots with swoops, etc. His next letter was entirely in his secret code. While those letters are lost, and the code forgotten, I still remember how much fun it was to 'crack the code' and then write letters to him in his secret code."

I was so taken with this idea that I created a code and sent a coded message to my two young grandsons. I pulled out the idea again recently when friends were visiting with their third and fourth-grade children. They latched onto the code immediately, and by the end of the evening, not only had they deciphered the coded messages I had written them, but they had sent me their own. I've posted a sample on this book's resource page.

Karen shared another idea for engaging children: custom-made crossword puzzles. Make up your own clues and answers based on the child's age and interests. Use graph paper to make it look real and let the answer words intersect occasionally. Then put the clues below. Be sure to keep a copy yourself in case they get stuck and turn to you for help.

In her wonderful book *How to Write Heartfelt Letters to Treasure: For Special Occasions and Occasions Made Special*, Lynette M. Smith includes many terrific ideas and occasions for engaging with children of all ages. She encourages readers to celebrate birthdays, of course, but also first or last days of school, graduations, going away to college, and other religious and secular events in the children's lives. Her chapter on childhood initiation rites for different cultures is worth the price of the whole book. She gives ideas for not only what to say but creative ways to present your note or letter.

Encouraging your children (or grandchildren) to write notes will pay off in the future when they grow up and move away and start writing those wonderful notes to YOU.

Notes as Creative Expression

I once read about a note sent to a professional baker. The stationery was a recycled bag of flour. The baker responded with a note written on a cut-out bag of sugar!

My brother-in-law Andy is wonderful about spontaneously sending a book he thinks I'll like and he always encloses a personal note inside the book's cover. The unspoken message is that he cares what I think and believes the book will give pleasure or provoke thought or conversation. It is a thoughtful, loving gesture, and whenever I pull the book off the shelf, I know it contains a written hug inside.

I've written notes on napkins, paper towels, brown kraft paper (on a roll or cut out of brown paper grocery sacks), and vintage postcards purchased at yard sales. You can make your own postcards by cutting off the decorative fronts of fold-over notecards you have received. Other oddball materials could include fabric or wallpaper sample swatches. Type "unusual stationery" into Etsy and see what comes up. Natural materials might include leaves or leather. The challenge is often finding a pen or marker that works on your material.

Don't be afraid to unleash your inner child and make your note writing an adventure in creativity. That said, the postal service is not keen on any material or artistic frill that would keep the piece of mail from going through their machinery, so be careful not to make them too bulky or irregular.

If your creativity lies in the visual arts more than writing, think beyond the emoji and put those gifts to work by adding your own sketches or drawings to enhance your words—or to replace them altogether. The Smithsonian Archives of American Art contains hundreds of illustrated letters from many famous American artists.

Artist Janice MacLeod took this idea to a whole new level in writing illustrated letters to subscribers about her experience in Paris. The entire collection is now available in her book *Dear Paris: The Paris Letters Collection.*

Self-Therapy

L ife can throw unexpected obstacles into our best-laid plans and activities. We might sustain an injury that keeps us sidelined with limited mobility and renders us bored to tears in a chair or bed. We might live with someone who is chronically or terminally ill, the pace of our days slowed down to a crawl as we sit with them to lend the comfort of our presence or be there in case they need help. We can read, of course, but reaching out to others through correspondence can be a calming and therapeutic way to while away some of those hours that might otherwise seem lost. If you can't get out to buy stationery, ask someone to bring it to you. Or get creative with pens and paper you might find on hand. There are relationships that can be nourished through personal note writing, even in those restricted situations.

In researching this book, I found many examples of writing letters to yourself as a form of catharsis, processing, or healing. This can be simple journaling, but some prefer to write to themselves a note or letter as if they were writing to a beloved friend. Beth Acker has written movingly about her struggles with mental illness, and she found that writing to herself was a powerful way to step back and see herself as a friend would see her and give herself advice that she needed desperately but wasn't getting from others in her life at the time. I came across examples of letter writers who wrote to their younger, wounded selves to help them move past childhood abuse or trauma.

Writing a letter to your future self can be an effective way to create or manifest a reality for yourself that hasn't happened yet. Much like goal setting, writing to yourself about what you want your life to be like, look like, or feel like several years from now—getting as specific as possible about your personal life, career, spiritual maturity, family— can create momentum toward that vision. Tuck it away and reread it every year to take stock and adjust accordingly.

The Forever Letter

Author Elana Zaiman coined the term "forever letter" in her inspiring book *The Forever Letter: Writing What We Believe For Those We Love*. It is a special kind of letter in which you share your values, wisdom, and love with one or more loved ones. While my book is primarily about notes rather than letters, the idea behind the forever letter is grounded in the Heartspoken principles of living, so I wanted to include it here.

According to Zaiman, the idea is inspired by the medieval Jewish tradition of the ethical will, a document parents wrote to their children, sharing their ideas and wishes and the ways they hoped their children would live their lives. But in *The Forever Letter*, she envisions a much more flexible and robust idea that might include a letter to a parent or friend or a teacher who has helped or inspired you. It might even be a letter to repair a broken relationship.

This kind of letter does not have to be done on your deathbed. It can be written any time and might be inspired by a life milestone such as the wedding of a child or your retirement. In fact, a forever letter can be a series of letters (or notes) on different topics of importance to you. Or it can be a letter you add to over time.

Writing a forever letter is also an effective way to get to know yourself and appreciate the values and people who have meant the most to you in your life. Zaiman's book includes ideas, prompts, and heartwarming guidance for writing your own Forever Letter.

Notes for Posthumous Delivery

W ho wants to think about writing a note or letter for delivery after your death? At first glance, this seems morbid, and why write to someone if you won't be around to know their reaction? Years ago, Debbie Gruber contributed an article to my blog that shifted my thinking on this. Debbie remembered taking an overseas trip without her children. Sitting in the plane, she felt overwhelmed by the desire to tell them how much they meant to her in case she never made it home. This got her thinking about how much she would love to have a note or letter from the loved ones in her family who had died.

When my young cousin Carlyle was diagnosed with late-stage cancer, she knew she was unlikely to survive. In the face of her mortality, she wrote many notes and letters to her young children to be given to them on their birthdays and other milestones for years to come. They were part of the legacy she wished to leave them.

Perhaps you need to make an apology you haven't made in person, but you can't bring yourself to do it in your lifetime. A note of apology can feel cathartic, even if the other person won't see it right away.

Or perhaps you were once hurt and have been unable to let it go. Your imminent death might bring you to a change of heart. You might want to write, *"I forgive you,"* and ask that your note be delivered later.

Letters You May Never Mail

A note or letter doesn't have to be mailed to be worthwhile or therapeutic.

Historian Doris Kearns Goodwin, in *Leadership in Turbulent Times*, described a tactic Abraham Lincoln used for self-control during his turbulent presidency and the Civil War. When he was angry with anyone—politicians, his military leaders, or colleagues—he wrote a letter expressing his rage, but he always put it aside at least a few hours or overnight. He waited until he could revisit his words in a calmer state of mind, and he rarely sent the letter. Years after his death, these letters were found with his notation: *"Never sent and never signed."*

I was deeply moved to read about high school teacher Elena Aguilar who worked with emerging writers for whom English was their second language. After hearing a student speak of her sense of abandonment and shame from her father's severe mental breakdown after his brutal treatment years before in a Cambodian prison camp, the teacher suggested the student write a letter to her father. He had become a street person who didn't even know her, shouting to imaginary prison guards and fellow prisoners. The exercise was so therapeutic, the teacher encouraged all her students to write letters to people from their past—letters they would never mail. The response was overwhelming, the teacher recalled:

"They wrote . . . They wrote to fathers who abandoned them, to parents who were in jail, to grandparents in rural villages in foreign countries, to relatives who died, to older brothers trapped in gangs, to parents who worked long hours or drank too much or just couldn't understand their teenager."

Grief therapists often encourage their patients to process their sadness with pen and paper. Consider whether you could cleanse yourself of pent-up emotion, resentment, sorrow, hurt, and anger by writing a letter to someone, living or dead. You may never mail these letters, but they can still be amazingly healing. Or maybe you will mail one (or more) and reestablish a connection you thought was lost forever.

More Words for
Difficult Situations

There are many situations so difficult, sad, devastating, or unimaginable that words will never be enough: suicides, accidents, the death of a child, a cancer diagnosis, a relationship betrayal, a scandal. Don't let the difficulty or awkwardness keep you from reaching out and connecting in the smallest way. You may have a chance to do more later, but when you first learn of this kind of situation, sometimes the kindest and least intrusive way to connect is with a note.

- Words are totally inadequate, but I wanted to reach out and let you know you're not alone.

- Words fail me, but I had to send a hug by mail during this awful time.

- There is no explanation for this tragedy. My heart is broken for you.

- Every fiber of my being wants to swoop in and make things better for you, but for now, just know I hold you in my heart.

- I know there must be a Susan-shaped hole in your heart right now and the pain is unbearable. In my mind's eye, I am holding you close and hoping you may soon be comforted by loving friends and happy memories.

My Most Unusual Notes

Embarrassing, Awkward, or Tragic

Friends and family members can get themselves into a heap of trouble. But even if their actions were awful or embarrassing or hard to forgive, it can be important to reach out in kindness. You can do this without condoning the alleged actions, and they will remember your gesture vividly because so many other friends and acquaintances—often responding to limited news or gossip—will be distancing themselves.

My archives include notes to:

- a church friend arrested for driving under the influence of alcohol.

- a relative whose wife asked him to leave until he could control his drinking.

- a friend accused by an employee of improperly spying on them.

- a community leader during some highly publicized and embarrassing financial difficulties.

- a relative who had been imprisoned.

✒ A widower after his wife was savagely murdered.

I don't expect a response. I rarely learn if my note helped or not. One exception was the note I received from a business owner to whom I had written when I learned he was facing bankruptcy. He responded, *"Ms. Cottrell, I truly appreciate the encouraging letter you sent me during one of the most difficult and testing times of my life. I'm certain I read your note over more than twenty times. It was a lifeline which kept my spirits up."*

Life can turn on a dime, and we could be the ones suffering from shame and humiliation. When we can offer grace to others, we should do it.

Political Civility

We live in a rural area where we personally know most of our civic leaders and politicians. Though I rarely write letters to the editor of our paper, I write to local leaders both when I support them and when I disagree with them. Our county elections can sometimes be contentious, with candidates ending up dirty from all the mudslinging. More than once, right before such an election, I wrote to candidates urging them to rise above the fray and remember that if elected, they will represent all the citizens in their district, not only the ones who voted for them. If more of us reached out in this way to local, state, and national politicians, perhaps it would encourage a greater level of civility than we see today.

Welcome to Womanhood

When my niece—and godchild—was about to turn thirteen, my precious sister asked me and some of her closest women friends to write her daughter a "Welcome to Womanhood" letter in celebration of the physical and spiritual transitions she was experiencing. I would never have thought of writing something like this on my own, but it gave me a chance to think about this special threshold in a young woman's life and share what wisdom I might impart. I wrote many things, but the letter ended this way:

> *"You already have everything you will ever need—the intelligence, the knowledge, the courage, and the power—to do what God intends for you to do in this life. Your job, as you grow and mature, is to believe in yourself and learn to trust your instincts and your heart. I love you."*

CHAPTER VI
Take It to the Office:
Business and Professional Notes

"You glance at an e-mail. You give more attention to a real letter."

~ Judith Martin

Your Heart Belongs in Your Business Too

When an action benefits both parties, we have the quintessential "win-win," and that is how I view the practice of note writing in business. Personal notes—especially handwritten ones—are overlooked communication tools for busy professionals. When they're not included in your success toolkit, you're missing out on a unique opportunity to make a positive impact on your professional relationships, letting them know you care about them and reminding them of your thoughtfulness and your genuine desire to serve them. Most of the tips throughout this book are applicable to professional notes as well as personal ones.

My brother, Bruce Herbert, told me about an experience he had as a rookie financial consultant with Merrill Lynch in the 1980s. He was assigned a client who—because she was known to be talkative and a bit of a complainer—had been passed off to several fledgling rookies over the years. She had legitimate questions about her portfolio, so Bruce spoke with her at length and promised to get back in touch with a response. Wanting to personalize the experience, he researched the situation and composed a handwritten note thanking her for her business and summarizing what they had discussed. The managing partner was furious when he found that Bruce had sent a handwritten note instead of one typed on formal office letterhead, declaring it unprofessional and inappropriate. But after receiving Bruce's letter, this lady called the office, asked to speak to the manager, and showered him with praise for having advisors who would take the time to send a handwritten, clearly personal-to-her letter that made her feel so valued. That manager never critiqued Bruce again for handwriting notes, and the lady became a quite enjoyable client, which makes the story's lesson clear. When the occasion calls for it, your clients and customers will love getting handwritten notes and letters precisely because they are human and not machine made.

In all the rhetoric about work-life balance, there has emerged the unfortunate notion that we can compartmentalize our work life from our personal life. In the most fundamental ways, however, I don't believe we can do this, at least not for long. What affects us in one area will invariably bleed over into the other. The same goes for note writing to clients, customers, employees, and business associates.

Recently, several entrepreneurial circles have engaged in lively conversations about how to run a "heart-centered business." I am delighted to see this and believe heartspoken notes can play an important role in your professional life and success.

But I can hear the outcry now, the "I don't have time!" No, you must *make* time as many highly successful men and women have done. Douglas Conant, CEO of Campbell's Soup Company between 2001 and 2011 is said to have written 30,000 personal handwritten notes to his 20,000 employees. *"My work philosophy—my life philosophy,"* said Conant, *"is to be tough-minded on standards and tenderhearted with people."* And President George H.W. Bush wrote personal notes almost every day. Clearly, these men could be Heartspoken ambassadors.

Set an example for your employees and business associates. If you have an onboarding program for your new hires, especially sales professionals and executives, make sure they know how to use personal correspondence to nurture their relationships. Give them a copy of this book when they join your team and make note writing easier for them by keeping them supplied with plenty of your organization's letterhead and notecards. Equipped with such stationery, all they need to do is add a brief message and address the envelope. Every one of the cards they send to a client or prospect is a connection with your company.

As board chair for First Bank here in the Shenandoah Valley, I try to send personal notes (emails too) to employees for milestone dates and achievements or when they have had a death in their family. I've received touching feedback about how much this means to them to know they are not just a number in the organization, but a real person.

Remember the Secret NOTES Formula

The acronym NOTES I discussed in chapter III can often be applied to professional notes as well as personal ones, especially when you're doing more than signing your name on a preprinted card. Your employees, associates, and clients will notice and appreciate a personal note for one main reason: they rarely get one. Here is the formula again, adapted for your professional use:

N for Natural:

Write naturally, as though you are speaking in person. This is no time for flowery or effusive phrasing that could be construed as insincere.

O for Open:

Before you start writing, take a few seconds to *open* your mind to your own innate wisdom. Be clear about your intention, think about the person to whom you are writing, and consider the outcome you want your note to have.

T for Tell:

Don't beat around the bush; *tell* the person what you want to say and what you want them to think, do, or feel as a result of reading your letter. A professional note is rarely the place for clever humor or subtle references.

E for Empathize:

Empathize with the receiver as best you can, especially when you are sending condolences or responding to a difficult situation. How would you feel if you were the other person reading your words? When you identify and feel what you want the outcome to be, the words will flow more easily.

S for Share:

Sharing—such as a specific memory, observation, or compliment—is even important in a professional note. If you're writing to an employee, tell them exactly what they did to merit your praise. Or if you're writing to a client, tell them why you appreciate them or their trust in you for your products or services. We've all gotten far too many generic, computer-generated notes and letters. Make yours stand out with details that will be meaningful to the reader.

It's important to remember that business notes aren't the same as personal notes. While the principles are the same—and gratitude or sympathy are certainly universal emotions—there are ways in which a business note should differ from a personal note:

- *"Sincerely"* or *"All the best"* (the late President George H.W. Bush's favorite) are more appropriate closing phrases than something more personal.

- Keep the content relevant (stick to the facts) and avoid getting too flowery.

- Keep the tone professional to ensure your words won't be misconstrued as inappropriately personal or affectionate.

- It's sometimes okay to enclose a business card. You wouldn't do that in a personal note.

It's All About Connection

Connection is the secret sauce of any successful business, and this involves cultivating your professional relationships. These relationships are likely to be in one of three categories: clients, customers, prospects; employees; and business associates inside and outside your office. A fourth, more temporary, category of professional relationship is the one between job applicants and those who interview them and make hiring decisions.

1. Clients, Customers, and Prospects

When I receive a personal communication from someone with whom I've done business, I feel seen, heard, and appreciated. It increases my sense of confidence at having chosen to give them my business. It's rare to receive acknowledgment of my transaction, so when I get one, it stands out. I also welcome the reminders of their products and services, especially if they include a business card to make it easy for me to make future purchases. A personal note keeps you and your company on that person's radar screen. Here are a few messages to consider:

- Thanks for coming in.
- Thanks for your purchase and assurance of continued service.

- Happy birthday.
- Here's an upcoming sale or event that might interest you.
- I'm following up to make sure your _____ meets your needs.

I got this handwritten note from a professional consultant who helped me:

> *"Thank you for the opportunity to serve you. I consider it a privilege and a blessing to be a small part of your writing journey. Please consider referring me to your friends. I will send you a token of my appreciation."*

From a financial advisor, we received this handwritten note:

> *"Please know that my appreciation for your business goes far beyond its financial significance. I am grateful for your trust and assure you we will continue to earn it by giving you the best possible service."*

Being on the receiving end of a good sales or service experience gives you the opportunity to not only let them know what a good job they did but also refer them to others. For example, a downsizing company recently did an outstanding job helping me clear, vacate, and clean the apartment of an elderly friend who had to quickly move to a nursing home. In appreciation, I sent a note and their business card to the executives of two local retirement communities to suggest they add this company to their residents' resource list.

2. Employees

Take the time to write your employees personal notes, and they will notice and appreciate your effort. Here are some reasons you might do that:

- Congratulations on an award or promotion
- Sympathy for a personal loss
- Happy birthday wishes or recognition of a life milestone or achievements of family members
- Acknowledgment of good work, good project, sales success, etc.
- Acknowledgment of a work milestone: years with the company or organization
- Recognition of their role in a company achievement

Look for chances to pass on third-party compliments to an employee, even when you didn't observe or experience it yourself. These are powerful affirmations to let an employee know they are highly valued:

> *"Jenny, your supervisor told me how hard you worked on the recent production project and how much your attitude kept everyone excited and productive. Thank you for being such an important part of our organization's success."*

Whenever you write a personal note of praise or recognition to an employee, add a photocopy to their file so anyone in a future supervisory or human resource role can see this employee was recognized for superior performance.

3. Business Associates

You never know when another professional might be able to send business your way. They're more likely to think of you if you've done the same for them or if you've stayed in touch. A sincere note is such an easy and effective way of staying top of mind with those who matter in your professional life.

Making a new contact at a social or networking event is a perfect opportunity to follow up with a note; be sure to enclose your business card and a mention of where the contact was made. Other messages you might convey in a note to a fellow professional are:

- ✎ You might be interested in this book/article/event.

- ✎ Thank you for your insights.

- ✎ Thanks for referring Mary to me.

- ✎ Thank you for meeting with me. I appreciated your time.

- ✎ I'd like to introduce you to . . .

- ✎ It was nice to see you at the chamber event.

- ✎ Welcome to our area. I'd be glad to take you as my guest to this upcoming event.

- ✎ I appreciated your time in speaking with me.

4. Job Applicants

One important tool for professional networking is the follow-up note after you've been interviewed for a potential job position. Here's an instance where I suggest using both email *and* a handwritten note. The email is a quick expression of your gratitude for the interviewer's time and your enthusiasm for the position. The personal note is what could seal the deal, because not many other candidates will bother to write one. My friend Karen confirmed this from her own experience. She said, *"After my interview for an administrative assistant position with my local university, I sent a handwritten note of appreciation. I got the job and learned later I was the only one of several candidates who had bothered to send a personal note."*

Even when you don't get the job you wanted, a note written after an interview can sometimes make enough of an impression to open the door for other positions in the company.

Holiday Card Tips for
Business Owners

"It takes very little these days to stand out from the crowd. Sincere courtesy and simple kindness are like a bright light in a dark room."

~ Lydia Ramsey

"**T**hanksgiving, Christmas, Hanukkah, and Kwanzaa are among the great reasons to connect with your customers and prospects during the holiday season," says international business etiquette expert Lydia Ramsey. Ms. Ramsey has given me permission to share her holiday card tips to ease the chore and to make your best impression:

> "Planning is always a good idea, but too often most of us leave things to the last minute. One of the victims of procrastination is the holiday card. In your business and your personal life, if you wait too long to start the process—like after Thanksgiving, sending your cards may become more of a chore than a pleasure. If you delay, your clients and colleagues may already have left the office for the holidays and your friends may be too swamped at that point to notice your thoughtfulness.

> ✦ **Purchase a quality card.** *It is not necessary to spend a fortune, but good quality says you value your clients, colleagues, and friends enough to 'send the very best.'*

- ***Order your cards while there is time to have your name or the company's name printed on them.*** *You want them to have a professional look.*

- ***Send your greetings early.*** *Have them in the mail the first week in December if you want them to be noticed and appreciated.*

- ***Plan to sign your name and write a brief message.*** *The holiday card that comes without a personal signature and a note seems more obligatory than celebratory. It does not matter that your name is already printed on the card. Give it that handwritten touch.*

- ***Address the envelopes by hand.*** *While it is easier and faster to print address labels, you lose the personal touch. Consider hiring someone to do this if you do not have the time to do it yourself.*

- ***Use titles when addressing your cards.*** *The envelope should be addressed to 'Mr. John Smith' not 'John Smith' or 'Ms. Mary Brown' not 'Mary Brown.' By the way, 'Ms.' is the correct title to use in business.*

- ***Invest in holiday stamps and avoid the postage meter.*** *This is one more personal touch—and a festive one at that.*

- ***Email greeting cards may be tempting because they require less time and trouble.*** *It is not totally in bad taste these days to e-mail your holiday wishes, but it is impersonal and not the most impressive way to do it. Your clever electronic message with singing Santa and dancing trees is a fleeting greeting. The recipient will click on the URL, download the card, open it, read it, smile, close it, and, in all probability, hit 'delete.' Chances are good that your physical card will have a longer lifespan. Most people save greeting cards throughout the holiday season, and many display them around their office or home.*

- ***One final tip: Address your envelopes as soon as you receive your cards.*** *Once you get that step out of the way, you can sit back and relax while you write your personal message on each greeting card.*

Special Advice for Nonprofits and Fundraisers

"The best way to find yourself is to lose yourself in the service of others."

~ Mahatma Gandhi

Effective nonprofit leaders and fundraisers know how important it is to make genuine connections with donors and prospects. The development and nurturing of these relationships is not done quickly or easily but through repeated contact and skilled listening. In this way, you learn what tugs at a donor's heartstrings (and purse strings), and you can show how your nonprofit organization or charitable cause could be the best vehicle for their dreams and generosity. Connection is always a two-way proposition, and these individuals will appreciate that their gift makes a difference in the world or your community.

Personal—and often handwritten—notes to both past and prospective donors should be a crucial piece of your outreach efforts. As we enter the third decade of the twenty-first century, much of our nation's disposable wealth is in the hands of baby boomers who grew up being taught that handwritten notes were not only nice but expected. Even to their children and grandchildren who are inheriting or earning this wealth, such efforts are still noticed. It is only human nature to appreciate anyone who reaches out in a personal way.

Don't limit your note-writing outreach to your organization's executive director. Encourage board members to contribute to development efforts by writing to their own personal connections to actively promote the organization and ask for support.

Here is a letter I wrote to a couple who made an unusually large donation to a nonprofit on whose board I served. One of them was also a member of our board:

> The receipt of the year-end statement of your donation prompts me to thank you once again for the remarkable generosity and commitment you have demonstrated to our community and our organization. I truly believe your gift has jump-started us years beyond where we would have been without it.
>
> As if this wasn't enough, there is absolutely no way I can ever express my gratitude for your tireless commitment to us in your capacity as board member. I rely regularly on your good judgment, your experience, and your gentle way of keeping me grounded. And on those days when it seems like it's all too much, I think about how far we've come and how much effort, faith, and vision have been invested.
>
> As we enter the beginning of the next decade of service, I am more optimistic than ever that we can move confidently toward the goals we know you share with us. Thank you.

Here are a few opportunities for writing a note to your supporters and prospects:

- When there is news about the causes or projects they have supported

- To invite them to a talk or program in which they might be interested

- To share a book or movie you think they'd like

- To share good news about your organization or your work

- To congratulate them on a personal accomplishment or milestone

- To recognize the accomplishments of their family members, especially children or grandchildren

- To ask their advice on a topic in their area of expertise

- To request an introduction to someone you think might help you

As with any heartspoken note, take a moment before you write to connect, heart and mind, with the person to whom you're writing. Their engagement with you and your cause is often as meaningful to them as it is to you. They will be glad you wrote.

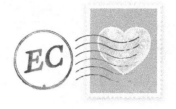

CHAPTER VII
Tools of the Trade

"You have all the tools right now to make this day, this moment, happy. The best of these tools is love."

~ Neale Donald Walsch

Any artist knows the tools they use affect the quality of their finished work. Writing notes and letters is no exception, and when you take the time to create the right space and equip it with quality tools, you'll be so much more likely to use it and enjoy yourself. Links to many of the items I use or mention below—and more—can be found on the book's online resource page.

A Place to Write

If you have the luxury of a dedicated space in your home—perhaps a small desk and chair with a good light—you can easily keep all your supplies close at hand and have a place to write your notes comfortably and happily.

I have a desk my grandmother gave me, but often I enjoy writing notes in my sunroom where I keep a pen holder with my favorite pens and use a lapboard with a drawer where I can keep a few writing supplies.

Some of the members of my Facebook group "The Art of the Heartspoken Note" (https://facebook.com/groups/HeartspokenNotes) bought little caddies to hold their basic supplies: stationery, pens, stamps, address book. The caddy can be tucked out of sight or easily carried around the house or out to your deck or patio—wherever you want to write your notes.

Address Book

I used to have an address book with soul-nourishing art depicted on the cover. Through the years, as my friends and I moved, it became messy with crossed-out addresses. I eventually decided to make the plunge to digital. Now I have joined the modern world in keeping my address book on my iPhone. It's too darned convenient. For those who still like going old school, check the online resource page for links to some lovely address books.

Correspondence Journal/Record Book

The more robust your correspondence life is, the more important it is to have a place to record what you mail. This serves two purposes. One is simply a place to look if you can't remember whether you sent that note you've been thinking about for so long. The second is to have a record in case your intended recipient doesn't receive what you mailed and you need to verify when you mailed it. This can be especially helpful for bill payments or professional correspondence.

If you're intentionally trying to write more notes, keeping a record is an encouraging way to monitor your progress. I use my journal for all outgoing mail. It has three simple columns: two narrow columns for the date and a code and a wider column for the recipient's name and other details. My personal codes are below, but use codes that make sense to *you* so you'll remember them:

- $$: Bill payment or donation
- BD: Birthday
- CG: Congratulations
- CH: Christmas
- EN: Encouragement
- GW: Get well
- NY: New Year's
- O: Other
- SY: Sympathy
- TH: Thank you
- TY: Thinking of you

✒ On-the-Go Essentials

One secret to writing more notes is to always be prepared with supplies at your fingertips. A very small mobile pack can be as simple as a Zip-Loc bag big enough to hold a few cards and envelopes, one or two pens, and some stamps. This is handy when you find yourself waiting for an appointment or meeting. Clear or fabric zippered bags might also be perfect, especially if they fit inside your purse, briefcase, or tote bag. Write those notes while you're waiting in the dentist's office and mail them before you get home.

✒ Paper, Paper, Paper!

Beautiful paper is a visual and tactile treat. Choosing the right stationery can seem as important as choosing the right words. The selection gets more diverse every year. From the chic and sophisticated designs at Crane & Co. to the beautiful florals at Rifle Paper Company or the sassy collections curated by Mail More Love, it's easier than ever to find stationery to suit your style.

I have friends who can't resist buying shoes or clothes. My guilty pleasure is lovely stationery, especially if it's unique in design, color, or texture. I'm in heaven if you take me to a store that sells papers, pens, notecards, and journals. I'm always on the lookout for quality, discounted stationery products, especially in high-end shops. Even my local Wild Birds Unlimited store has racks of notecards with exquisitely depicted birds and nature scenes. They almost *call* to me! Don't forget to check out your local discount stores. They often have amazing prices on special-occasion cards or specialty card packs from brand-name companies.

Some of my favorite artists offer stunning notecards featuring their work: Meriah Kruse, Lori Portka, and Mickey Baxter-Spade. From art museum shops, you can find stationery featuring art and designs of every imaginable style. And of course, the internet is your best friend if you love stationery. I've gotten some amazing and original cards from artists on Etsy.

If you use a fountain pen, make sure it's compatible with your stationery. Lots of beautiful artwork cards use glossy cardstock because it's best for showing off the art, but fountain pen ink may smear on them. If you purchase sheets of paper or a journal, make sure the paper is sufficiently heavy so your fountain pen ink won't bleed through. I keep an assortment of fountain pens, gel pens, and rollerball pens to make sure I have what I need for any given paper or card stock.

You'll find links for paper and stationery on my online resource page (see the URL at the back of this book). I've also been a supplier for Carlson Craft and Navitor for years, so if you need personalized stationery, holiday cards, wedding invitations, or special event invitations, contact me through my website contact page. I'll be happy to help you with your personal or professional stationery needs.

Writing Implements

Until I got serious about writing notes, I had no idea there was an entire subculture of pen aficionados in the world. I am now on catalog lists for stores selling pens—mostly fountain pens and ballpoint pens—that range from under twenty to thousands of dollars, depending on their intricacy, their materials, and the uniqueness of their design and issue. There are also pen holders and display cases for the avid collector. Who knew? Go to YouTube and search for "fountain pens" or "fountain pen reviews" and you'll find hundreds of videos telling you in the minutest detail about how each pen can affect your writing experience.

You don't need to spend a fortune on writing implements, but be sure to consider comfort and functionality as well as appearance. Some pens fit your hand better than others, so if you're going to invest in a quality fountain pen, you should go to a store where you can hold them and write with them.

Unless you use a fountain pen regularly, it will soon dry out and must be emptied and cleaned before it can be used again. I have four nice fountain pens (with a different color ink in each) and several Pentel EnerGel (rollerball) pens in various colors. These rollerball pens write like fountain pens, but on certain kinds of paper, they don't bleed through as much as fountain pen ink.

If you'd like to explore the topic of writing implements further, the links on this book's resource page (https://www.heartspoken.com/heartspoken-book-resources) will get you started.

Inks

If you are a connoisseur of fountain pens, you are likely to become a connoisseur of inks too. As with pens, YouTube is a treasure trove of videos about different brands and types of inks.

And oh, the colors! The selection of ink colors available is amazing, and some companies sell little samples, each tube holding enough for about one pen filling. This is such a fun way to give them a try before buying a whole bottle.

Rollerball pens and some ballpoint pens can be less messy and more affordable alternatives to fountain pens. I recently discovered PILOT FriXion erasable, refillable pens. They write so much more smoothly than the early erasable pens and they're also available in many colors. If you want to be able to erase your mistakes when you send handwritten notes, this might be a good option. Of course, they're not as permanent as standard ink and should never be used for signatures or legal documents, but for most purposes, they are sufficient. I especially love erasable pens for my Bullet Journal and kitchen calendar for logging entries that are subject to change.

Stamps

The choosing and application of a postage stamp to your note can be a routine necessity or part of your creative process. The US Postal Service has a wonderful array of colorful and interesting stamps (even scratch-and-sniff stamps which are great for writing to children), and they issue new ones throughout the year. My friends Sherley and Ann suggested that the USPS website (usps.com/addstamps) is the best place to find a wider selection and buy the newer issues, because they often sell out quickly in local post offices. Vintage postage and discontinued Forever stamps are very popular and often sold on Etsy.

Considering how well a stamp looks on your envelope is important, but choose well. Be careful not to use a whimsical or political stamp on a sympathy note or other professional correspondence.

Do-It-Yourself Ideas

If you are the least bit crafty or artistic, you can add another dimension to your note writing with sketches, drawings, or garnishments of colors, shapes, or sparkles. The Smithsonian published a marvelous book of illustrated letters from their Archives of American Art. These missives include everything from detailed drawings to lipstick impressions and whimsical maps or directions.

I have friends who make their own paper and envelopes, and then add marvelous artistic touches for style and flair. Others recycle/repurpose all kinds of paper to make cards: magazine pictures or the fronts of cards they've received. Others use rubber stamps, stickers (scented or unscented), washi tape, and vintage postage stamps from yard sales to decorate their papers and envelopes. Any store selling scrapbooking supplies will offer templates for drawing shapes and letters. My grandsons have taught me the joy of stickers as a simple way to adorn my notes, letters, and even my journals. It's also fun to play around with sealing wax and seals (which you can buy customized with your own favorite motif or initial).

Please spare your recipient the frustration of spilling glitter all over themselves. I avoid buying Christmas or holiday cards with glitter because they make such a mess on my desk even before I've sent them off.

In the reference section, you'll find a link to an envelope template. You can use it to make your own envelopes out of anything from grocery sacks to wrapping paper.

CHAPTER VIII
Passing the Torch

"At my age . . . people often ask me if I'm 'passing the torch.' I explain that I'm keeping my torch, thank you very much—and I'm using it to light the torches of others."

~ Gloria Steinem

B orn in 1950, I may be among the last generation of human beings who grew up when physical mail was the lifeline of personal communication. When I was young, long-distance calls were expensive and infrequent. I well remember as a young adult when I got—reluctantly, I might add—my first fax machine, my first email account, and my first cell phone. Now I am young at heart, if not in age, and even before the pandemic reminded us of the joy of staying in touch with each other, I felt an urgency to share my passion for writing notes and letters.

I have taken to heart what my friend and author Steve Leveen, founder of Levenger, said,

> *"We are the living history of handwritten notes—those notes we received as children from our elders and the notes we sent back. It falls to our generation to carry the torch forward, to show the younger and the youngest how the old form of taking pen to paper still burns bright and carries a warmth all its own."*

Each of us can do just a little to keep this light burning. Happily, there are several young people who have shared my enthusiasm for promoting personal, handwritten notes. Hannah Brencher, Lea Redmond, Ivan Cash, Samara O'Shea, Shannon Hood, Kelsey Crowe, and Emily McDowell, I thank you, from the bottom of my heart.

If recent times have taught us anything, it's that time is too precious to waste. So, when you think about writing a note to family, a friend, or a complete stranger, don't wait. Do it.

And always—always—make it heartspoken.

Appendix A
Frequently Asked Questions

When friends, family, and readers of my blog learned I was writing a book on how to write notes, many had questions. I'm sharing the most frequent ones here. I hope my answers will support and encourage you in your own note-writing life.

Q: Is there a difference between notes and letters?

A: Practically everything I've offered about handwritten notes is equally true for letters. The letter is simply a longer form of expression allowing more detailed sharing or explanation. In personal correspondence, letters between two people can become almost a shared journaling of lives.

Letters, of course, take more time. In this fast-paced world of short attention spans, I felt a focus on notes rather than letters would be more helpful and more practical. If you have an interest in letter writing, though, read about some of the famous letter writers and letter writing as an art and a craft. I've included great resources in the appendices.

Q: **Is there ever a time when I don't need to send a thank-you note for a gift received?**

A: The etiquette experts at Emily Post say you can forego the handwritten thank-you note when you open the gift in person and thank them for it then (except for gifts received at a bridal or baby shower). But when you think of a thank-you note as a gift of love, you realize it's always a wonderful thing to do.

Q: **Does my note have to be handwritten?**

A: No, it doesn't. My grandfather's cherished stack of notes and letters to me were almost all typed on his old manual typewriter. I can see them from where I sit right now, and they inspire me.

   I type faster than I can write by hand, so sometimes I type a note or letter, print it, and mail it. I often choose this instead of email, especially if it contains content they might want to keep or file and because it's still nice to get real mail in your mailbox. For very personal notes—especially sympathy notes—handwritten is still the most meaningful and intimate.

   There are many reasons you may be unable or unwilling to write your note by hand, including mobility or pain issues. I hope my message in this book is clear: when we communicate from our hearts, regardless of the medium used, we are making a more powerful impact than we would otherwise. Handwritten notes are more personal and more intimate, but a heartspoken message can be conveyed in any form.

Q: **Can't I call or text instead of writing a note?**

A: Of course, you can do either, and sometimes that's the best way to convey your sentiment quickly and effectively. You can also do both. When a close friend is suffering from a sudden loss, I often call them right away and write a note for them to receive a day or two later.

   Phoning, texting, and email—especially between close

friends and colleagues or for less significant communications—are all preferable to not reaching out at all. Sometimes, you don't have time or access to pen, paper, or stamps. In that case, expediency may prevail over what's ideal.

When you've had dinner at the house of a friend whom you see often, a call may be the most appropriate option, especially if you don't want to obligate them to write to you after frequent get-togethers. But if it was a special occasion or required an unusual amount of effort or thoughtfulness on your host or hostess's part, a handwritten note is always appreciated.

There's a place for both calling and writing in most relationships. Think about your purpose, your time restraints, and your desired outcome. Words over the phone can be heartspoken too.

Q: Can you give me a little more guidance on when it's okay to give verbal thanks instead of written?

A: As far as thank-you notes, an expression of gratitude in any form is better than none. When deciding how to express your gratitude, consider the value of the gift, your relationship to the person you wish to thank, and how often you see them. Another variable might be the frequency of the gift. If your grandmother sends you twenty-five dollars every month, for instance, you should let her know by email or phone after each gift, so she'll know you received it, but an annual or occasional handwritten note of appreciation would probably suffice.

Handwritten notes between close friends who see each other often may be waived—especially for small or casual gifts. The important point is to make sure they understand, in some way, how much you appreciate their generosity.

Listen to your heart on this and always go back to the outcome you want to have or the impression you want to make. Do whatever it takes to accomplish that.

Q: My hand hurts! What other options do I have for sending handwritten notes?

A: If you can't write notes because of physical discomfort, you're not alone. In surveys I sent out to learn what kept respondents from writing handwritten notes, the most often cited culprits were disability, cramping, or pain from holding a pen or pencil. Happily, there are some marvelous digital note-writing services available today, and their quality has improved tremendously over the last few years. They not only look like real handwriting, but they also use quality paper stock and are surprisingly affordable when you consider the cost of stationery, stamps, and time. Assuming you can type on your computer's keyboard, these can be a wonderful alternative to handwritten notes.

If you sign up for a free account, you're given card and style options depending on the occasion. You can choose from several handwriting styles and then select size, line spacing, and ink color. Graphics are often optional. Some of these services are more geared toward corporate personal correspondence, so poke around until you find the one that suits you the best. I've provided links to some digital services in appendix D.

Q: What's a "Bread and Butter" Note?

A: Despite the odd name, a bread-and-butter note is a brief thank-you note to someone who has recently provided hospitality: a thank-you note from guest to host for a meal, a party, or an overnight stay.

You know how much trouble you go to when you're the one providing hospitality—even for a casual gathering. Preparing for a dinner party or overnight guests involves hours of planning, cleaning, cooking, and entertaining. Think about how much your host or hostess will love receiving a warm message mentioning the specific things you enjoyed about your time with them. They will know the effort they made on your behalf did not go unappreciated. Here's a lovely note I received after hosting a party for fellow board members and their spouses:

> *"Thank you so much for opening your home to us for the cocktail party on Friday. We really enjoyed spending the time to get to know others on the 'team' on a more personal level. It was such a special thing for you to do, and we had a great night! Thank you."*

And here's another excerpt from David, a friend of our son-in-law, who spent the night with us while he was in the area on a business trip:

> *"Please accept my sincerest appreciation and gratitude for welcoming me into your home, introducing me to the beautiful Shenandoah Valley, and sharing your favorite restaurants."*

As you gather your thoughts to write your hosts a bread-and-butter note, you will enjoy once again the pleasure of the time you spent in their company.

Q: How should I send thanks when a gift is given to both me and my spouse—or to the whole family?

A: If your spouse is a note or letter writer, you can share the writing. John and I, for example, both write notes for Christmas gifts we've received jointly. With sympathy notes, if he had a closer relationship with the deceased, he will write the note. Most of the time, though, I write sympathy notes on behalf of both of us by using "we" throughout or adding "John joins me in expressing our deepest sympathy to you and your family." Some newlyweds decide to divide post-wedding thank-you notes by guest, depending on which spouse invited them. If they are mutual friends, it's fine for each to include a message in the same note. Another option, of course, is for one person to write the note from both of you and include two signatures.

Families with young children often encourage their children to draw a picture or write their own message to be enclosed in the adult's note. This teaches them that the receipt of a gift calls for an expression of thanks.

Q: How long should my thank-you note be?

A: Some etiquette sources suggest a thank-you note must have four sentences:

1. Appreciation for the gift
2. Why you like it
3. How you'll use it
4. Closing sentence (e.g., "Looking forward to our next visit.")

But I consider this a guide, not a rule. One of the sweetest thank-you notes I ever received was from a club president after a fundraising event. He simply wrote,

"Thank you. We couldn't have done it without you."

Your note doesn't have to be anything other than what your heart and instincts tell you. Its content—and its length— should be motivated only by love and/or a genuine desire for authentic connection. Consider these short messages. Assuming the recipient knows to what you're referring, simple lines in your handwriting on a nice piece of paper or card can absolutely stand alone:

You're the best! Thank you.

Your kindness meant the world to me. Thank you.

You are amazing! I'm so proud of you.

Q: **What should I say when I don't like or want the gift received?**

A: I'm smiling as I think about an internet meme of a cat with a disgruntled frown on its face. The caption reads, *"I have to write a thank-you note for that? KEEP IT!"*

We've all been there. The Heartspoken way to handle this situation is to look past your feelings and focus on the intention of the giver, using words to describe them instead of the gift itself: generous, thoughtful, kind, etc. You can say you appreciate the bracelet even if you know you plan to recycle it to the local thrift shop. Perhaps you can honestly say it was unique or remarkable.

See page 52: "Pretend You're in Hollywood."

Q: **What if I'm too busy to write personal notes?**

A: You must *make* the time. All your other important activities must be prioritized, and this is no exception. If you don't *want* to make time for this, that's fine, but you should be honest with yourself and acknowledge it's your choice, not the fault of your busy schedule. Many prolific note writers are busier than you and I are ever likely to be. I've written about this issue in greater detail on my blog: "Too Busy to Write Personal Notes?" (https://www.heartspoken.com/3005/too-busy-to-write-personal-notes/).

Q: **If children aren't learning cursive, will they be able to read our handwritten letters in the future?**

A: Some school systems did drop the mandatory teaching of cursive, opting instead for manuscript writing, often also called "printing." Happily, educators tell us that if a cursive letter is written clearly, the letters are still identifiable and readable, even to someone who has only learned manuscript.

It is mostly a matter of legibility. I was taught cursive, but there are still many letters from others written in cursive that I find illegible. Historians have long struggled with illegible words in many of our early American documents and their unique cursive flourishes.

When my grandchildren get old enough to read, I may learn to adapt my own writing so they can read it more easily, whatever form that takes. Regardless, I will always make it heartspoken.

Q: **One of my pet peeves is when someone's note answers a question or comment I made in my earlier note to them without referencing it or reminding me what exactly they are responding to. I don't keep a copy of what I've sent people, so their out-of-context response sometimes leaves me wondering what they're talking about. How do you handle it?**

A: This is annoying, and I hope readers will pay attention to this and always make sure to be clear if you are answering a question or responding to a comment in a previous piece of correspondence (or even an email or phone call). As far as how to handle it, if I really can't figure out what they're referring to, I just pick up the phone and either blame it on my age or get cranky with them about their lack of clarity.

This might make a good case for keeping copies of your correspondence sent and received. I usually staple or paperclip my response to their original note or letter before filing it away.

On a side note, I have the same reaction to telephone

callers who start talking without telling me who they are. Not everyone has caller ID or instant voice recognition.

Q: **How can I find a mailing address when so many people have cell phones that aren't listed with an address in phone books?**

A: This is definitely a challenge, but here are some ideas to get you going:

- Whitepages.com is often helpful if you know their name and the city they're in. They have both a free and paid service, but I find the subscription fee is reasonable, and the service is good for finding both addresses and phone numbers.

- If you know where they work (corporate office, school, etc.), you can send a note care of that organization and often they will get it.

- If the person went to the same college or high school as you, the alumni/alumnae office may be able to find addresses for you.

- Do they have a website? If so, there might be a mailing address listed. There is almost surely a contact form you can use to ask them for an address.

- If you find a listing for the person's agent or publisher, you can sometimes contact them and ask them to forward your note. Be sure to include postage and an envelope.

- If all else fails but the person has a social media presence, you can scan your note and send it as an attachment to a private message.

APPENDIX B
Note-Writing Lists, Checklists, and Printables

To view, download, or print any of the following, visit this book's online resource page: https://heartspoken.com/heartspoken-book-resources:

- **The Secret NOTES Formula**
  This is the essence of my book: a formula you will use over and over to find your own voice and always write notes that comfort, connect, encourage, and inspire.

- **12 Note-Writing Tips: A Checklist**
  Keep this handy guide close at hand for your general note writing.

- **Heartspoken's Thank-you Note Checklist**
  Once you've used this list a few times, writing a beautiful, heartspoken thank-you note will become second nature.

- **Heartspoken's Sympathy Note Checklist**
  Sympathy notes require special handling. This checklist will help you write a note that will comfort and avoid common mistakes.

✒ **Sympathy Note Insert**

Print this insert on cardstock to tuck into your sympathy notes when you want to add a special message.

✒ **Sample Correspondence Journal Page**

This can be printed on a standard page size (8-1/2" x 11") or a smaller size (5-1/2" x 8"), either of which can be bound or put into a notebook. Or use it as a guide for the page design of your own choosing. I draw columns in an A5 medium journal. Links to this and other journals can be found on the online resource page.

✒ **A List of Holidays by Month**

If you like to use holidays as a reason for writing—or an amusing mention in your notes—here's a list of a few of the many US holidays each month of the year. A printable list of holidays is included on our online resource page.

- **January:** New Year's, Chinese New Year, Epiphany, Martin Luther King's Birthday

- **February:** Groundhog Day, Valentine's Day, Presidents Day, Mardi Gras, Black History Month

- **March:** St. Patrick's Day, Spring Equinox, the Ides of March, Passover (date variable), Women's History Month

- **April:** April Fool's Day, Easter (date variable), Earth Day, Arbor Day, Ramadan (date variable), National Note and Letter Writing Month

- **May:** Kentucky Derby Day, May Day, Cinco de Mayo, VE Day, Mother's Day, Memorial Day, Asian American and Pacific Islander Heritage Month

- **June:** D-Day, Flag Day, Juneteenth, Summer Solstice, Father's Day, Pride Month

- **July:** Independence Day

- **August:** V-J Day, National Watermelon Day

- **September:** Labor Day, Rosh Hashanah (date variable), Grandparents' Day, Oktoberfest, Autumnal Equinox, National Hispanic Heritage Month (September 15 through October 15)

- **October:** Columbus Day (or Indigenous Peoples' Day), Halloween, LGBTQ+ History Month

- **November:** All Saints' Day, Veterans Day, Thanksgiving, Native American Heritage Month

- **December:** Pearl Harbor Day, Winter Solstice, Christmas, Hanukkah (date variable), Kwanzaa, Boxing Day

Letter-Writing Holidays

- January 23 (John Hancock's birthday) is National Handwriting Day.

- The second week in January is Universal Letter Writing Week.

- April is National Card and Letter Writing Month.

- September 1 is World Letter Writing Day.

- December 7 is National Letter Writing Day in the United States.

APPENDIX C
Swipe File: Inspiration from Other Writers

Faithful Words of Encouragement

If you don't know what a person's faith is, resist imposing your own. Christian words of encouragement, for instance, would be meaningful to another Christian, but they might be like acid to an atheist. When you are sure of their beliefs, however, a quote from their scripture may be a great source for words of encouragement. Here are a few:

Christianity

"Anxiety weighs down the human heart, but a good word cheers it up."

~ Proverbs 12:25 (NRSV)

"I have said this to you, so that in me you may have peace. In the world you face persecution. But take courage; I have conquered the world!"

~ John 16:33 (NRSV

"Do not worry about anything, but in everything by prayer and supplication with thanksgiving let your requests be made known to God. ⁷ And the peace of God, which surpasses all understanding, will guard your hearts and your minds in Christ Jesus.

~ Philippians 4:6-7 (NRSV)

"So do not worry about tomorrow, for tomorrow will bring worries of its own. Today's trouble is enough for today.

~Matthew 6:34 (NRSV)

Judaism

"Do not worry thyself with the trouble of tomorrow; perhaps thou wilt have no tomorrow, and why shouldst thou trouble thyself about a world that is not thine?"

~ The Talmud

"Don't sell the sun to buy a candle."

~ Jewish proverb

"Don't take the burdens of the world's problems upon yourself. Don't ignore them either."

~ Babylonian Talmud

"The day you were born is the day God decided that the world could not exist without you."

~ Rabbi Nachman of Breslov

Islam

"Turn to Allah and you will find His Mercy heal every aching part of your heart and soul. Allah will guide you; He will bring clarity to your eyes, make soft your heart, and make firm your soul."

~ Anonymous

"So, lose not heart, nor fall into despair, for you will be superior if you are true in faith."

~ Surah Al-Imran 3:139

"In Him, hope is never dead. In Him, love is never lost."

~ Yasmin Mogahed

Buddhism

"It is better to travel well than to arrive."

~ Buddha

"The seed of suffering in you may be strong, but don't wait until you have no more suffering before allowing yourself to be happy."

~Thich Nhat Hanh

"The purpose of a rose is to be a rose. Your purpose is to be yourself. You don't have to run anywhere to become someone else. You are wonderful just as you are."

~ Thich Nhat Hanh

Native American

"Great Spirit, the good road and the road of difficulties you have made me cross; and where they cross, the place is holy."

~ Black Elk

"The Great Spirit is everywhere; He hears whatever is in our minds and our hearts, and it is not necessary to speak to Him in a loud voice."

~ Black Elk

"There is one God looking down on us all. We are all children of one God. God is listening to me. The sun, the darkness, the winds, are all listening to what we now say."

~ Geronimo

APPENDIX D
Additional Note-Writing Resources

Note-writing Services

For those with mobility impairments or who prefer writing with a keyboard, there are now services to help. The most affordable are the digital services that can produce notes and letters that look remarkably like handwritten notes. If you want to explore how to use these to up your correspondence game, I've included names below, and you'll find live links on this book's online resource page: https://www.heartspoken.com/heartspoken-book-resources. You can also find services to address your envelopes by hand or write your notes and letters. A local teenager with good penmanship might be thrilled to help you for reasonable compensation.

While the business section of this book (chapter VI) refers primarily to individual personal notes in a business context, some companies have embraced handwritten notes in their marketing efforts, and for good reason. From a purely practical standpoint, consider how readily different types of communication are opened and read. A successful email campaign is lucky to get a 20 to 30 percent open rate (the average is about 18 percent). Handwritten mail, on the other hand, enjoys a remarkable 90 to 99 percent open rate.

- Ballpoint Marketing (https://ballpointmarketing.com/) provides direct mail for real estate investors, agents, insurance companies, and nonprofits. They've designed robots to write with real ballpoint pens in blue ink.

- Cardly (https://www.cardly.net) lets you send a personal, handwritten card without lifting a pen. This online company has a wide selection of personal and holiday styles, and if you have overseas correspondents, you can save by having your cards shipped from the United Kingdom, Australia, or the United States. Use discount code HEART. I wrote about this company on my blog: https://www.heartspoken.com/13226/hate-to-write-handwritten-notes-cardly-to-the-rescue/.

- Handwrytten (https://www.handwrytten.com/) has a blog with great ideas for wording different kinds of professional notes and letters: https://www.handwrytten.com/resources/.

- Letter Friend (https://letterfriend.com/) offers real letters written by real people. They are geared more toward companies than individuals and offer both project pricing and subscription pricing. "Create more sales pipeline with real handwritten letters sent via web, API, CRM, and more. Handwritten cards, notes, & more. No Robots. Always Written by a Human. 100% Customized."

- Simply Noted (https://simplynoted.com/) offers notes that appear handwritten plus the ability to enclose a gift card from many major stores.

- Thankster (http://www.thankster.com/) can take a sample of your own handwriting and replicate it. They also have controls for font size and letter and line spacing so you can make their fonts unique.

- WAMI (https://wami.io/) has a mission to focus on providing high-quality, handwritten notes at scale to brands/companies to help them connect with customers in a more personal way than through emails.

- Write Way Notes (https://writewaynotes.com) allows you to choose your card, type your message, and have them do the rest to deliver what, for all the world, looks like a handwritten note or letter.

Business Etiquette Resources

- Business Culture website: https://businessculture.org

- Emily Post downloadable business etiquette tips: https://emilypost.com/advice/downloadable-business-etiquette-resources

- Formal Letter (https://formalletter.net/) is an interesting blog filled with samples and templates for various types of formal types of correspondence you might need, especially in your career or professional life.

- GCFGlobal business etiquette training: https://edu.gcfglobal.org/en/jobsuccess/business-etiquette/1/

- Lydia Ramsey (https://LydiaRamsey.com) is a Savannah-based business etiquette expert, professional speaker, premier trainer, and author. Her blog includes posts in business apology, email etiquette, sympathy etiquette, thank-you notes, and handwritten notes.

Famous Letter Writers

The number of famous letter writers through the centuries is legion. These are but a few to pique your interest:

- Persian Queen Atossa who, according to ancient historian Hellanicus, wrote the first handwritten letter around 500 BC.

- Pliny the Younger recorded the 79 AD eruption of Mt. Vesuvius in a letter to his friend, the historian Tacitus. His uncle, Pliny the Elder—also a great letter writer—died trying to rescue friends from Pompeii. His nephew recorded the uncle's bravery.

- St. Paul of Tarsus is the apostle credited with thirteen epistles in the New Testament. He is unlikely to have written them all, but he was clearly a prolific letter writer.

- The Venerable Bede, an eighth-century monk, wrote letters with vivid imagery and documentation of life in the Dark Ages. His letter to a bishop of the time detailed his view of monastic corruption.

- Horatio Nelson was Vice Admiral of the British Royal Navy and national hero in the late-eighteenth to early-nineteenth centuries, particularly during the Napoleonic Wars. He left thousands of letters, some of which have been invaluable to naval historians. Of wider appeal are letters—often lustful—he wrote to his mistress, Lady Hamilton.

- Queen Victoria mused in her letter writing on a wide range of Victorian England topics.

- Wilfred Owen, famous for his poetry from the WWI trenches, is also known for the letters he wrote to his mother about the horrors of war and the unique bonds forged between men suffering together in the trenches.

- Eleanor Roosevelt wrote daily impassioned and intimate missives to friends, family, politicians, and many leaders of the mid-twentieth century.

- President George H. W. Bush's handwritten notes were legendary in their number as well as their warmth and thoughtfulness.

Podcast or Video Episodes

- Jason F. Wright's story about a teacher's handwritten letter that changed his life after his father died: https://youtu.be/e2ad-fJK1Ik

- In an episode ("One envelope at a time") on the Meditative Story Podcast, Hannah Brencher speaks movingly about the impact of her mother's letters and has inspired many to take up their pen and write more notes and letters (https://podcasts.apple.com/us/podcast/id1472106563?i=1000455345959).

- "Uplifting the Heart with Handwritten Letters & Addressing Difficult Topics With Passion and Grace." In this episode of 88 Cups of Tea podcast, the host Yin Yang interviews Hannah Brencher (https://88cupsoftea.com/hannahbrencher/).

- Rhea Gaur speaks about "The Lost Art of Handwritten Letters and Cards." (https://ladybirdink.net/2020/08/28/the-lost-art-of-handwritten-notes-podcast/).

- Dan Lamothe. "Letters from war." A podcast from *The Washington Post*. This is a series of podcasts telling the story of four Eyde brothers in WWII—in their own words through their letters (https://www.washingtonpost.com/podcasts/letters-from-war/).

Blogs and Websites

- 365 Letters (http://365lettersblog.blogspot.com/). While not current, this website has some wonderful, archived posts about letters and letter writers. The author writes about letter writing, stamps, postcards, mail art, etc.

- Anchored Scraps (https://anchoredscraps.com/). This blog is dedicated to letter-writing enthusiasts and encouraging old-style correspondence through handwritten letters.

- From Me to You Letters (https://www.frommetoyouletters. co.uk/blog/). This blog is specifically aimed to help you write letters and notes to someone living with cancer.

- Lives of Letters: The Manchester Centre for Correspondence Studies (https://livesofletters.wordpress.com/). This organization's blog is for history buffs who might want to learn more about the past through the letters written by their ancestors.

- The Handwritten Letter Appreciation Society blog (https:// thehandwrittenletterappreciationsociety.org/). This is a membership organization in England dedicated to handwritten letters, but you don't have to be a member to enjoy their blog.

- The Pen Company (https://www.thepencompany.com/blog/). As the name indicates, this site sells pens as well as paper and inks. They also have posts in their blog that might help you enjoy your note and letter writing more.

- The Postal Store (https://store.usps.com/store/home). Here you'll find stamps, supplies, cards, and gifts to celebrate our appreciation for the US Postal Service.

- The Smithsonian National Postal Museum (https:// postalmuseum.si.edu). This is a treasure trove of information and history of our country's mail service. I can't wait to visit the museum in person.

- Write On (https://www.writeoncampaign.com/blog). This site chronicles a movement to encourage note, letter, and card writing.

Epistolary Novels

Epistolary novels are books in which the story is told through an exchange of letters or diary entries. Here's a great list: "100 Must-

Read Epistolary Novels From The Past And Present" (https://bookriot. com/100-epistolary-novels-from-the-past-and-present/). Some of my favorite epistolary novels (in order of publication date) are:

- *Dracula* by Bram Stoker (1897)
- *Screwtape Letters* by C.S. Lewis (1942)
- *Harriet the Spy* by Louise Fitzhugh (1964)
- *84, Charing Cross Road* by Helene Hanff (1970)
- *The Wednesday Letters* by Jason F. Wright (2007)
- *The Guernsey Literary and Potato Peel Pie Society* by Mary Ann Shaffer and Annie Barrows (2008)
- *Where'd You Go Bernadette* by Martha Semple (2013)
- *Meet Me at the Museum* by Anne Youngsen (2019)
- *The Lost Manuscript* by Cathy Bonidan (2021)

ACKNOWLEDGEMENTS

T his was the scariest part of the book to write, yet in so many ways, it's the most important. I've tried to be diligent about logging the names of dear ones I need to thank, but of course, there will inevitably be omissions. For those, I must simply ask forgiveness.

It is heartwarming to look back over the years and realize how many words of support and encouragement contributed to the overall project, often just when my doubts were high, or my energy was flagging. Even just a "How's your book coming?" meant the world to me. Thank you, each and all, for every one of those "hugs."

The first person I need to thank is my daughter Sarah Cottrell Propst. On my birthday right after the pandemic had shut down the world, she called and said, "Mom, you've finally got the time. I want you to get that book out of your head and onto paper." She then gifted me with several hours of time with a wonderful accountability coach Heather Wood Galpert, who called me weekly to get my progress report and see that I had set goals for the following week. That tangible proof of Sarah's belief in me was pivotal to the book getting written.

Next, I thank my dear friend, unofficial editor, and head cheerleader (and sometimes rear-end kicker) Karen R. Sanderson. Karen's unwavering belief in me and my vision for this book have been essential. When I was overwhelmed with getting the book finished and published, she stepped up as co-administrator of my Facebook group, "The Art of the Heartspoken Note," and made sure there was engaging content for the faithful members. She was both sounding board and idea generator through thick and thin, putting up with my crankiness and enthusiasm with equanimity. What a gift she has been!

The first professional editing of the book was done by the incomparable Shawn MacKENZIE. Shawn not only caught errors and omissions, but she went above and beyond our agreed-upon service to suggest rearrangements and rewordings that made the book so much stronger. If you ever need an editor, let me know, and I'll make introductions.

What a boost to my confidence when *New York Times* best-selling author Jason F. Wright agreed to write the foreword. He was completely slammed with his own book launch and nationwide book tour, but he believed in me and in the book's message, capturing it beautifully in his words.

Leading business etiquette and modern manners expert Lydia Ramsey graciously made a significant contribution to the book in chapter VI "Take It to the Office: Business and Professional Notes." Her enthusiasm for the project and willingness to lend her name and reputation to it were deeply appreciated.

Fellow author Lynette M. Smith also made a significant contribution to chapter V: "Outside-the-Box Note Writing" by allowing me to share a story from her own book about a special letter from her son and daughter-in-law on their wedding day.

I am sincerely indebted to my friend Clint Greenleaf, CEO of Content Capital in Austin, TX. On several occasions, he offered valuable insight and guidance that helped me navigate the complexities of the publishing industry. Whitney Gosset, the company's President, was also generous with her time and knowledge.

I belong to several groups whose members have been enormously generous in their support and enthusiasm for this book project:

- My local Shenandoah County WRITES group of fellow published authors: Cara Achterberg, Jim Davison, Mark Muse (a.k.a. Dana Hayward) and Coe Sherrard (a.k.a. E.A. Coe).

- My own Facebook group "The Art of the Heartspoken Note," whose members have patiently and enthusiastically been both cheerleaders and advisors. Many of the stories and quotes in this book came from our lively online conversations about heartspoken notes. Special shout-out to Beth Boland, Ellen Britt, Joyce Brooks, Jan Carroza, Lois Carter Crawford, Ann Davison, Dianne Frayne, Suzanne Artz McIlwee, Pamela McRae-Dux, Esther Hastings Miller, Katherine Morrison, Leslie Dunn Pace, Annette Petrick, Lydia Ramsey, Becky Russell, Sherron Racey Kamen, Mugogo Mark Stuart, Beth Vogt, and Jean Wise.

- The VECCA (Valley Educational Center for the Creative Arts) writers' group, especially Sarah Kohrs and Kara Garbe Balcerzak.

- The Wordsharks, a group of kindred writing spirits. I love you all: J J Brown, Jessica Messinger, Karen R. Sanderson, Shawn MacKENZIE, and Pamela Wight.

- The Best Yet Writers, an online group of "mature" writers who share our writing journeys with each other, especially Sarah Christy, Anna Burch Evans, Terha Knittel, Joy Newswanger, Doris Swift, Sally French Wessely, and Cindy LaFavre Yorks.

- Your Platform Matters: an online membership group led by writing coach Ann Kroeker, who has taught me so much about content creation and heart-centered marketing.

- Marketing Trailblazers: an online membership group led by Denise Wakeman. Denise has been a coach, mentor, and friend, most recently in planning and executing my book launch. Her co-administrator Jan Carroza has also become a friend and has sent me so many helpful articles and tips. Special thanks also to fellow members Ellen Britt, Luc Dermul, Sue Guiher, Meriah

Kruse, Sue Painter, Vicki Peel, Kim Ravida, Judy Rodman, and Laura E. West for their generous comments and sharing of my content.

In the "random acts of kindness" category, I want to thank Connie Ragen Green. She is a legend in the world of online entrepreneurial coaching, and a multi-book author in her own right. I met her at a conference several years ago and wrote a handwritten note to thank her for what she taught me. Many months later, out of the blue, she remembered a conversation we'd had and sent me a book about note writing that is right in front of me on my shelf of books on the subject. Gestures like this convey the unspoken message: "I think note writing is important too."

Warmest thanks to Pamela McRae-Dux, a high school classmate and fellow author, whose frequent handwritten notes and a beautiful journal book all conveyed the message, "You've got this."

I'm so grateful to everyone who sent me a testimonial for the book. Thank you, in advance, to all of you who will, hopefully, leave five-star reviews on Amazon and Goodreads.

Sincere thanks to my two tech support gurus: my webmaster and friend Nancy Camden and Danielle Koehler, who designed a new home page to focus on the book's launch.

The staff at Koehler Books has been terrific, especially John Koehler, Miranda Dillon, and Lauren Sheldon.

I am blessed to have such a supportive family. My brother Bruce T. Herbert and his wife Nancy provided several timely gestures of support and feedback, especially the gift of a course on book writing and some stories and quotes that I used in the book. My sister Sarah C. Albritton and her husband Andrew LaRowe were ever ready to provide feedback and encouragement.

My husband Dr. John A. Cottrell, Jr., besides his unflagging support for the book and his help as a beta reader and cover judge, has picked up many extra household chores over the last two years to give me time to write and focus. I love you and appreciate you so much.

The words in this book have been steeped in prayer. One beautiful August morning—in the "messy middle" of writing this book—I was feeling overwhelmed and asked God for motivation and guidance. As clearly as if it were a spoken voice, I heard the still small voice of his Holy Spirit: "I need you to equip my people with this powerful tool for sharing my love and encouraging each other."

Thanks be to God and to God be the glory.

BIBLIOGRAPHY

Acker, B. L. "To Myself, When Recovery from Depression is 'Sink or Swim.'" The Mighty website (October 13, 2016): https://themighty.com/2016/10/writing-a-letter-to-yourself-for-when-youre-depressed/.

Aguilar, Elena. "Encouraging Students to Find an Audience When They Write." Edutopia website (December 6, 2011): https://www.edutopia.org/blog/writing-for-an-audience-strategy-elena-aguilar.

Bender, Heide. *A Modern Guide to Writing Thank-You Notes.* Scotts Valley: CreateSpace, 2016.

Bowler, Kate. *Everything Happens for a Reason: and other lies I've loved.* New York: Random House, 2018.

Brencher, Hannah. "Letters to strangers." TED Talk (June, 2012): https://www.ted.com/talks/hannah_brencher_love_letters_to_strangers.

Brittanica.com. "Paper." https://www.britannica.com/technology/paper.

Brittanica.com. "Parchment." https://www.britannica.com/topic/parchment.

Bush, George. *All the Best, George Bush: My Life in Letters and Other Writings.* New York: Scribner, 1999.

Cash, Ivan. *Snail Mail My Email: Handwritten Letters in a Digital World.* Naperville: Sourcebooks, Inc, 2012.

Cottrell, Elizabeth H. "From Papyrus to Paper: A Journey Through History." Heartspoken blog (undated): https://www.heartspoken.com/2609/papyrus/

Cottrell, Elizabeth H. "3 Letters That Changed History: Letter Writing Day Dec. 7." Heartspoken blog (undated): https://www.heartspoken. com/7475/3-letters-changed-history-letter-writing-day-dec-7/.

Crowe, Dr. Kelsey and Emily McDowell. *There Is No Good Card for This: What To Say and Do When Life Is Scary, Awful, and Unfair to People You Love.* San Francisco: HarperOne, 2017.

Edge, Simon and Julie Carpenter. "History's greatest letter writers." *The Express* online (May 25, 2010): https://www.express.co.uk/ expressyourself/177014/History-s-greatest-letter-writers.

Ensminger, Angela and Keely Chace. *Note-Worthy: a guide to writing great personal notes.* Kansas City: Hallmark Books, 2007.

Fuller, Neathery Batsell. "A Brief History of Paper." St. Louis Community College website (2002): http://users.stlcc.edu/nfuller/paper.

Garfield, Simon. *To the Letter: A Celebration of the Lost Art of Letter Writing.* New York: Gotham Books, 2013.

Gaudet, John J. *The Pharaoh's Treasure: The Origin of Paper and the Rise of Western Civilization.* New York: Pegasus Books, 2018.

Hamadey, Gina. *I Want To Thank You.* New York: TarcherPerigree, 2021.

Haugk, Kenneth C. *A Time to Grieve.* St. Louis: Stephen Ministries, 2004, https://www.stephenministries.org/griefresources/default. cfm/774.

Haugk, Kenneth C. *Experiencing Grief.* St. Louis: Stephen Ministries, 2004, https://www.stephenministries.org/griefresources/default. cfm/774.

Hewat, Katie. *Thinking of You: A Card Greeting for Every Occasion.* Heatherton: Hinkler Books, 2010.

Isaacs, Florence. *Business Notes: Writing Personal Notes That Build Professional Relationships.* New York: Clarkson Potter/Publishers, 1998.

Isaacs, Florence. *Just a Note to Say …:The Perfect Words for Every Occasion.* New York: Clarkson Potter/Publishers, 2005.

Isaacs, Florence. *My Deepest Sympathies: Meaningful Sentiments for Condolence Notes and Conversations.* New York: Clarkson Potter/Publishers, 2005.

Jones, Malcolm. "The History and Lost Art of Letter Writing" *Newsweek* online. (January 17, 2009): https://www.newsweek.com/history-and-lost-art-letter-writing-78365.

Jordan, Brenna. *The Lost Art of Handwriting: Rediscover the Beauty and Power of Penmanship.* Avon: First Adams Media hardcover edition, Adams Media, 2019.

Kirwin, Liza, et al. *More than Words: Illustrated Letters from the Smithsonian's Archives of American Art.* New York: Princeton Architectural Press, 2005.

Lamb, Sandra E. *Personal Notes: How to Write from the Heart for Any Occasion.* 1st ed, New York: St. Martin's Press, 2003.

Lamb, Sandra E. *Write the Right Words: Messages From The Heart For Every Occasion.* New York: St. Martin's Press, 2010.

Leek, Andy. "Notes to Strangers project" in London: http://www.andy-leek.com/notes-to-strangers.

Lerner, Harriet. *Why Won't You Apologize?: Healing Big Betrayals and Everyday Hurts.* Manhattan: Touchstone (Simon & Schuster, Inc.), 2017.

Lewis, Georgia. "Christmas cards stitch up the threads of a lifetime." *The Washington Post* website (December 27, 2009): https://www.washingtonpost.com/wp-dyn/content/article/2009/12/26/AR2009122601724.html.

Leyba, Erin. "Thanking Others is Actually Good for YOU, Research Confirms." *Psychology Today.* (May 7, 2016): https://www.psychologytoday.com/us/blog/joyful-parenting/201605/thanking-others-is-actually-good-you-research-confirms.

Littauer, Florence, et al. *A Letter Is a Gift Forever: The Charm and Tradition of a Handwritten Note.* Eugene: Harvest House Publishers, 2001.

Lopez, Rozanne. "Handwriting—a love story." Author's blog (December 7, 2014): https://rozannelopez.com/handwriting-a-love-story/.

MacLeod, Janice. *Dear Paris: The Paris Letters Collection.* Kansas City: Andrews McMeel Publishing, 2021.

MacLeod, Janice. *Paris Letters: A Travel Memoir about Art, Writing, and Finding Love in Paris.* Naperville: Sourcebooks, 2014.

Marie, Jenna. "What to Write in Business Sympathy Cards." Simplest Sympathy website (August 11, 2013): https://simplesympathy.com/business-sympathy-cards.html.

Merrick, Julie. *A Letter A Week: Your guide to writing and mailing 52 handwritten letters during the year.* Olympia: Julie Merrick, 2021.

O'Shea, Samara. *For the Love of Letters: A 21st-Century Guide to the Art of Letter Writing.* 1st ed, New York: Collins, 2007.

Page, Sydney. "As a child, she wrote to a WWII vet. He carried the letter everywhere, and 12 years later, they finally met." *The Washington Post* website (September 14, 2021): https://www.washingtonpost.com/lifestyle/2021/09/14/wwii-vet-letter-child-war/.

Petrow, Steven. "Joe Biden's wise words about death helped me understand the realities of life." *The Washington Post* (June 2, 2015): https://www.washingtonpost.com/posteverything/wp/2015/06/02/joe-bidens-wise-words-about-death-helped-me-better-understand-the-realities-of-life/.

Petrow, Steven. "Pen, Paper and Sympathy." *AARP Bulletin*, April 2021.

Pen Heaven. "Handwritten Letters Which Made History. Pen Heaven's blog, undated: https://www.penheaven.co.uk/blog/handwritten-letters-which-made-history.

Piedmont Healthcare. "Therapeutic Benefits of Writing Letters." Piedmont Healthcare website, undated: https://www.piedmont.org/living-better/therapeutic-benefits-of-writing-letters.

Ramsey, Lydia. "The Etiquette of Sympathy: When a Colleague or Client Suffers a Loss." Lydia Ramsey's Business Etiquette website (May 20, 2016): https://lydiaramsey.com/etiquette-of-sympathy/.

Rueb, Emily S. "Cursive Seemed to Go the Way of Quills and Parchment. Now It's Coming Back." *The New York Times* online, April 13, 2019: https://www.nytimes.com/2019/04/13/education/cursive-writing.html.

Sankovitch, Nina. *Signed, Sealed, Delivered: Celebrating the Joys of Letter Writing.* New York: Simon & Schulster, 2014.

Sennett, Jay. "An Introduction to Handwritten Notes & Correspondence." *Gentleman's Gazette* website: https://www.gentlemansgazette.com/handwritten-notes-correspondence/.

Shepard, Sam, and Johnny Dark. *Two Prospectors: The Letters of Sam Shepard and Johnny Dark.* Edited by Chad Hammett. Austin: University of Texas Press, 2017.

Shepherd, Margaret. *The Art of the Handwritten Note: A Guide to Reclaiming Civilized Communications*. 1st ed. New York: Broadway Books, 2002.

Smith, Lynette M. *How to Write Heartfelt Letters to Treasure: For Special Occasions and Occasions Made Special*. Yorba Linda, CA: All My Best, 2012.

Spizman, Robyn Freedman. *When Words Matter Most: Thoughtful Words and Deeds to Express Just the Right Thing at the Right Time*. 1st ed, New York: Crown Publishers, 1996.

Stoddard, Alexandra. *Gift of a Letter*. New York: Avon Books, 1991.

Thornton, Tamara Plakins. *Handwriting in America: A Cultural History*. New Haven: Yale University Press, 1996.

Trubek, Anne. *The History and Uncertain Future of Handwriting*. London: Bloomsbury Publishing, 2016.

University of Michigan, The. "Papyrus Making 101: rediscovering the craft of making ancient paper." (2004): https://apps.lib.umich.edu/papyrus_making/pm_intro.html.

Usher, Shaun, compiler. *Letters of Note: An Eclectic Collection of Correspondence Deserving of a Wider Audience*. San Francisco: Chronicle Books, LLC., 2017.

Victoria Magazine (editors). *Writing Personal Notes & Letters*. New York: Hearst, 2003.

Waxel, Marie. "Letters of gratitude: Unexpected notes for North Alabama WWII vet." WAAY TV website (October 1, 2021): https://www.waaytv.com/news/letters-of-gratitude-unexpected-notes-for-north-alabama-wwii-veteran/article_455f816c-b967-5617-aa70-a7af4b3558c8.html.

Webolt Company. "The History of Rice Paper." Company website (undated): https://www.rice-paper.com/about/history.html.

West, Laura. "The #JoySpark Mission project." Center for Joyful Business website (undated): https://www.joyfulbusiness.com/joyspark/.

Williams, Jennifer, editor. *Victoria, the Pleasures of Staying in Touch: Writing Memorable Letters.* 1st ed. New York: Hearst Books, 1998.

Wright. H. Norman. *What to Say: When You Don't Know What to Say.* Eugene: Harvest House Publishers, 2014.

Wright, Jason. "Jason tells a story about a handwritten letter that changed his life." YouTube. August 31, 2009: https://youtu.be/e2ad-fJK1Ik.

Wright, Jason. "There's something special about letters." *Northern Virginia Daily* (April 6, 2020): https://www.nvdaily.com/nvdaily/jason-wright-theres-something-special-about-letters/article_6db38c32-874b-5092-9220-1fbfd8aa641e.html.

Zaiman, Elana. *The Forever Letter: Writing What We Believe For Those We Love.* Woodbury: Llewellyn Publications, 2017.

ADDITIONAL RESOURCES ON THE HEARTSPOKEN WEBSITE

GO HERE (https://www.heartspoken.com/heartspoken-book-resources/) for a wide range of ideas and free downloads (checklists, printables, templates).